TopGear
TOP DRIVES

ROAD TRIPS OF A LIFETIME IN THE
WORLD'S MOST DRAMATIC LOCATIONS

FEATURING

NORTH POLE CHALLENGE, LAMBO IN THE FAROE ISLES, STUART HIGHWAY, FERRARI IN PERU, ASTON IN ITALY, JAG ACROSS THE STATES, DISCOVERY IN NEPAL, SMART IN LAPLAND, MERC IN TRANSYLVANIA, MONDEO IN RUSSIA, FERRARI THROUGH CHINA, iCAR ROUND JAPAN, LAND CRUISER IN NAMIBIA, FERRARI IN NORWAY

W9-BOO-716

Chapter 7.

Chapter 5.

Chapter 17.

Chapter 14.

Chapter 13.

Chapter 19.

Chapter 1.

Chapter 11.

Chapter 15.

Chapter 9.

Chapter 18.

Chapter 16.

Chapter 8.

Chapter 6.

Chapter 10.

Chapter 10.

Chapter 2.

Chapter 3.

Chapter 12.

Chapter 4.

CONTENTS

FOREWORD BY
JEREMY CLARKSON

In this book there aren't any tours of back roads that take
you past the ancient settlements of Wales. You won't find
James and Oz trundling towards you along the sleepy
vineyard lanes of France. These are *Top Gear* drives, and
they're quite unlike any other. The standard grade-A road trip
involves a great road and an Italian supercar, and you get that,
even if it's as fantastically pointless as taking an F430 all the
way to Norway so we can hear its V8 bounce off the tunnel
walls. But *Top Gear Top Drives* goes further, bringing you the
most unusual combinations of car and tarmac
from all across the planet.
A long drive for the sake of a long drive is one of the great
pleasures of life, but trust me it doesn't need to be on the
Stelvio Pass in a Gallardo Superleggera. Well, actually, it does
help a lot if you're in a Lambo in the Alps, but just read our
journey of a sales rep's Mondeo bouncing along the shit roads
of Russia, and you'll know exactly what I mean. So read this,
then grab your keys and hit the road – phone off, your music,
your route, your timetable. Enjoy that pleasure before
somebody makes it a guilty one.

Jeremy Clarkson

INTRODUCTION BY
MICHAEL HARVEY

For once around here, it's not all about the cars.
Between these covers you'll find adventure, endeavour, jeopardy, bravery,
stupidity, self-discovery and, of course, more than one Sunday-evening celebrity.

Top Gear Top Drives is our first collection of travel and adventure stories
inspired by *Top Gear*'s unique relationship with cars; think of it as
'Around the World in (not quite) 80 Drives'.

There's more than one way to judge a car's merit. Around here we reckon the more it
inspires you to do, the further to drive, the harder it has to prove itself, the greater the
mountain to climb (yes, literally), the better the car is. So get set for Ferraris across
China, Jags across America and a little car with no doors, windows, roof or heater all
the way to the Arctic Circle. That story alone is worth the purchase price of this book.

If you're not familiar with *Top Gear* magazine, then you might not be familiar with
some of the names reporting from every continent except Antarctica
(well, leave us something for next time...). Rest assured, they've all been through
the *Top Gear* school and come with Mr Clarkson's recommendation. They have
some great stories to tell you, and some great cars to share, too.

Michael Harvey. Editorial Director, *Top Gear*

Chapter 1

Our friends in the north

When Jeremy Clarkson, Richard Hammond and James May decided to head to the North Pole, the first problem was deciding which one. And that was just the beginning

Words James May Photography by Polar bears

THE FUNDAMENTAL PROBLEM with any journey to the North Pole is that there are, in fact, two: the Magnetic North Pole, which is a physical phenomenon, and the True North Pole, which is a cartographical convention established from the shape of the Earth and the axis of its rotation. Bored yet? This is only the beginning.

You might wonder why this is. Well, the Magnetic North Pole is useful for most basic navigation as it determines the direction of a compass needle. Unfortunately, it moves around a bit over the years, and severely buggers up map-making. Also, for the purposes of dividing the globe into lines of longitude, which relate to time as well as position, the True North Pole is better because it's right at what we think of as the 'top' of the planet. Serious maps are oriented towards True North, and if navigating with a magnetic compass, as most amateur sailors and airmen do, it is important to allow for something called 'magnetic variation'; that is, how many degrees away from True North your Magnetic North is. This changes around the planet and is indicated on maps using something called 'isogonal lines'. In London, for example,

magnetic variation is currently about 3 degrees west. Bloody hell.

It's important to establish which North Pole you are talking about when using an expression such as 'let's go to the North Pole'. Technically, if you are at the North Pole, everything is south, no matter which way you turn. If you are at the Magnetic North Pole, then True North Pole is to the south, and if you are heading to the Magnetic North Pole and find yourself at the True North Pole, the North Pole is still to the North. Unless, that is, you are working to true bearings, in which case you will stand at the True North Pole with your magnetic compass still pointing north, but actually that's south.

Anyway, we decided to head for the Magnetic North Pole; or rather, Clarkson and Hammond did. Clarkson, the best off-road driver in the world, would go in a Toyota pickup truck, and Hammond would eschew at least a century of progress and be towed there by some dogs. I didn't actually want to go at all. I hate snow, I hate extreme cold, I hate dressing up and I knew it would involve quite a lot of camping, since there are no hotels around there.

ARC

< >

NORTH POLE MISSION

Vehicle: Toyota Hilux
Climate: A bit parky
Distance: 833 miles
Duration: Far, far too long
Road Surface: White
Roadkill Roulette: Fortunately none of the huskies. Or Richard Hammond
Notes: The small matter of finding the North Pole, for no reason other than to say you've done it.

'Every night Clarkson would zip himself up in his sleeping bag and then blaspheme all night long. He was like a big sweary maggot'

This could be the Arctic from an aeroplane or at head height. No one knows

But Jeremy insisted, saying I should come along as his navigator. This was insulting, because navigating to the Magnetic North Pole is a matter of heading north with a compass. Even if, starting from Canada, I followed the wrong end of the needle, I'd know about it once we got to Mexico.

Now we have completed this great odyssey, I can categorically confirm

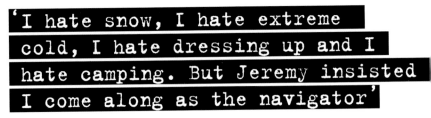

'I hate snow, I hate extreme cold, I hate dressing up and I hate camping. But Jeremy insisted I come along as the navigator'

that going to the North Pole, by whatever means, is a completely futile and miserable exercise. It starts with the special Arctic clothing, all of which is covered in stupid zips that catch in everything and makes a really irritating and deafening rustling noise if you so much as scratch your head. Doing a poo in the Arctic involves removing 10 layers of this stuff and then quite liter-

ally freezing your nuts off. And that's if you don't get eaten by a bear while your trolleys are down.

You might imagine that endless vistas of snow, interrupted only by abstract ice sculpture, is something quite beautiful to behold, and it is. For an hour or so. But after a few days it's a bit like looking at a screwed-up sheet of plain A4 paper. Open the freezer compartment of your fridge and look at that for two weeks to get an idea.

The extreme cold is a nuisance. Because the atmosphere is extremely dry up there, none of your personal effects ever freezes solid; they just become very cold. My favourite line from Jeremy: 'Ooh, this pillow's nice and toasty warm. No, hang on, what I meant was it's f***ing freezing.'

However, the instant you spill anything – your gin and tonic, say – then your trousers become part of the landscape. I took a packet of Johnson's baby wipes with me, for the purpose of 'washing', but within 10 minutes they'd become a scented iceberg. Only in the Arctic have I been presented with the problem of having to keep my tins of tonic warm enough to drink. And don't imagine that we were nice and warm in the car – we weren't allowed to have the heating on because it would interfere with our special misery-spec Arctic on-board cameras.

I hardly dare remind myself of the camping. It's not just that the tent had to be erected and dismantled every day, or that the zips on that always stuck as well, or even that the rudimentary

One of the many useful road signs to be found in the North Pole

kerosene stove set light to my face. The real problem was having to share it with Clarkson, who was incapable of helping to put the thing up, even though the job required the use of his favourite tool, a hammer.

I'm not a great camper, but Clarkson is a worse one. Every night he would zip himself up in his cocoon-style sleeping bag, even his head, and then blaspheme into the thick down all night long. It was like sharing a tent with a big sweary maggot.

There was little respite during the day, whatever the day was. Because it was the summer, the sun simply cavorted up and down the sky like

with the caviar and quails eggs I'd smuggled past the Arctic exploration Nazis, and he rewarded me by shooting my tin of Spam, for which I wish a virulent pox upon him still.

And when we arrived at the Pole, there was nothing. No monument, no visitors' centre. It was just more snow. We intended to leave a small *Top Gear* flag we had made, but discovered that we'd forgotten to bring the stick for it. With the mission accomplished, the doctor we'd taken along as part of our small support team asked me, 'So, James, now you've done it, do you think your life will be better for the experience?'

The North Pole is like 'crumpled A4 paper' according to James May

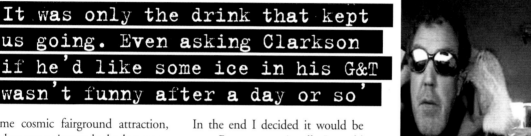

'It was only the drink that kept us going. Even asking Clarkson if he'd like some ice in his G&T wasn't funny after a day or so'

some cosmic fairground attraction, and at one point we had a huge row over whether it was lunchtime or midnight. We honestly didn't know. Driving was a simple matter of enduring the constant crashing and rattling of the overloaded Toyota, punctuated by the occasional dull report of another exploding tin of Schweppes as we crept further north (Magnetic).

I honestly believe that it was only the drink that kept us going. Even asking Clarkson if he'd like some ice in his G&T wasn't funny after a day or so. The conversation started well enough, with intelligent debate about politics and geography, but after a few days we were arguing for hours about the significance of just-in-time manufacturing versus the importance of interchangeability of parts, and by day four we had been reduced to food fantasies involving sandwich spread and sausages. I cheered Clarkson up

In the end I decided it would be worse. Because occasionally I would remember it.

It could be midnight. Then again, it might be lunchtime. Er...

Chapter 2

Discovery in the mountains

Driving through India is one of the most nerve-shredding experiences you can have. But make it to Nepal and you're cruising on the 'rooftop of the world'

Words Bill Thomas Photography by Steve Perry

PRECISELY HOW THE IDEA CAME ABOUT FOR THE TRIP BACK in 1964 remains a bit of a mystery. Dad reckons that Bob, with whom he worked at Rolls-Royce, walked into the office one day and accused him of leading a boring life, conveniently forgetting that his own life was almost exactly the same. Without delay, they'd both resigned and were on the road to Dover in a 27-year-old car, hand-painted white to reflect the heat, rear seats stripped out for extra luggage space, a big tent thrown in the back, spare wheel strapped to the roof and a Smith & Wesson .38 revolver in the door pocket.

When I was growing up in Australia, the final destination of Dad's epic journey, I heard a lot about Bob Claypoole, the Austin, and the drive to Kathmandu. Nepal seemed like the most romantic and remote place in the world to a young lad growing up in the suburbs of Brisbane.

The route went something like this: France, Switzerland, Italy, Yugoslavia, Bulgaria, Turkey, Syria, Lebanon, Jordan, Israel, Iraq, Iran, Afghanistan, Pakistan, India, Nepal. The Austin never missed a beat, broken axle aside. They didn't even suffer a puncture. Maybe, just maybe, it would still be up there.

Despite having lived in the UK for the last 17 years, I'd never met Bob Claypoole before our rendezvous at Heathrow to join photographer Steve Perry for the flight to Delhi. We were all laughing within seconds. Bob's like that, a big Bristolian with an even bigger sense of humour and an infectious,

The roads back in the 1960s were basic, but a lot less crowded than today

The Austin that took Bill Thomas' father to Nepal

<NEP

DISCOVERY TO NEPAL

Vehicle: Land Rover Discovery
Climate: Getting rather thin
Distance: 836 miles
Duration: 6 crazy days and nights
Road Surface: Dirt, tarmac
Roadkill Roulette: Thankfully, not any of us, but God knows how
Notes:
On the trail of an Austin lost back in the 1960s. Must remember never to drive in India ever again...

easy laugh. Dad, who flew into Delhi from Brisbane, hadn't seen Bob for 40 years before they shook hands in a scrappy hotel room near Indira Ghandi International, but of course it made no difference – they were soon laughing like old jackals, just like old times.

We set off from Delhi for Kathmandu by road, retracing the Austin's last steps. Rather than an ancient 40bhp 1600cc sidevalve Austin with semi-elliptic springs and an opening windscreen, we'd be on board a brand new Land Rover Discovery V6 diesel, shipped out there for us specially. When I asked for it, I couldn't think of a better vehicle for the job, and having done the drive, I still can't. In some of the most shocking and dangerous driving conditions in the world, and on some of the worst roads, the Disco wafted us along in safety.

I manoeuvered the big black 4x4 onto a Delhi road, objective Lucknow on the first night, 300 miles away. Our route would take us along Indian National Highway 2 to Agra, then across to Kanpur and Lucknow. From there, Dad and Bob followed the Ganges east to Patna on the original trip, but nowadays the border north of there is tense and difficult to cross, so we headed to Gorakhpur and entered Nepal further west at Bhairahawa. How times change

'How to describe the driving in India, as we avoided fatal accident after fatal accident? There really aren't the words'

– Dad and Bob pitched their tent wherever they liked, visas for each country were arranged at consulates in each country beforehand. Now, the idea of driving through Afghanistan and Iraq is unthinkable, and as we found out later, the Indian borders are riddled with corruption.

Neither of the senior travellers riding in the back seat had returned to India or Nepal since '64, and while Steve had visited in the 1980s, I'd never been and had no idea what faced me.

How to describe driving in India? The four of us discussed the problem in the Discovery, as I avoided fatal accident after fatal accident, and we agreed on this: you cannot effectively describe it. Impossible. God knows it was bad enough for me as the driver – it was so terribly dangerous I didn't dare let anyone else behind the wheel.

The only positive I took out of the Indian driving experience was to marvel at the sheer speed of human reactions when death is the consequence of a mistake or a brief lapse of concentration. Everyone on the road was concentrating hard – no nail polish drying going on here, no glancing in vanity mirrors or yapping on mobile phones. Just total concentration. And I was happy with my own driving, because no one died at my hand. This was nothing less than a driving test to the death. And just because we decided it was impossible to

The Indian concept of private space is a little different

A vision of paradise among the foothills of the Himalayas

The Land Rover Discovery was just the right car for the job

'Every vehicle blows its horn in India. It's actuall

encouraged on the back of trucks as good manners'

Every way you turn in Nepal
you find yourself a witness
to spectacular scenery

Lighting candles for
the *puja*, the prayers
traditional to Hindus

 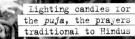

describe the experience doesn't mean I'm not going to try...

Here's one incident. Imagine travelling along a dual carriageway at 60mph in the fast lane, going around a blind bend and suddenly being confronted by a large truck coming straight at you, in your fast lane. What the f–? The truck flashed its lights at me, as if I'd done something wrong, then blasted by, his horn wailing. Every vehicle blows its horn constantly in India – it's encouraged with large signs on the backs of trucks, and is considered good manners.

What's going on? Why are you using my side of the road? And that was only one of many hundreds of near-fatal incidents we experienced on NH2. Check it out at topgear.com, where there are a couple of videos to watch. It's Hell.

We got out of India at midnight at the end of day two and what a blessed relief to be met at the Nepalese border by Sarad Pradhan from the Nepal Tourism Board. We were all in a state of semi-delirium as the Nepalese put garlands around our necks, unfurled a banner welcoming *Top Gear* to their country, and put cold Cokes in our hands. Civilisation at last. The final act from India was an attempt by corrupt border officials to extort bribes.

We drove a spectacular 175 miles from Bhairahawa to Kathmandu along the

> **'Dad and Bob remembered India in 1964 being like Nepal is now – that is, charming, fascinating quaint, beautiful and exotic'**

Narayani and Trishuni river valleys. This is a truly great road, well-surfaced and safe, bordered by sheer cliffs that the locals farm with amazing terraces. Dad and Bob remembered India in 1964 as being similar to Nepal now – that is, charming, fascinating, quaint, beautiful, exotic. It's a place where the people are bright-eyed and obviously proud of the communities in which they live.

There were exclamations of genuine surprise from the gents in the back when we rounded a ridge and set eyes on the Kathmandu valley for the first time. It's now about 50 times the size Bob and Dad remembered it – a small collection of temples and houses has now become a sprawling metropolis of 1.5 million souls. The full scale of the task ahead finally hit us – find an old Austin in that place? No chance, surely?

The hunt began in earnest the next day, when we met journalists from the *Kathmandu Post* and the *Kantipur*, the Nepalese national daily newspaper. We told them the story, gave them a picture of Dad with the car, and asked them to place a story in their papers asking people to ring in if they'd seen it or knew anything of it.

Later that day, we took the road to the old town of Bhaktapur, where the ancient centre and its narrow streets are preserved by law and the people's way of life is exactly how it's been for centuries. From there we went higher, up the

twisting road to Nagarkot, about 20 miles away. This road climbs and climbs up the valley side. It's a common misconception that Kathmandu is high, but in fact its elevation is 'only' about 4,300ft – it almost never snows there. But at Nagarkot we were up to 7,200ft and began to struggle for breath.

From Nagarkot, you gaze out to the east and on a clear day you can see the proper high country, across to mountains like Lhotse, Makalu and Sagarmatha (Everest), all well over 26,000ft. Sunrise from here is one of the world's most spectacular views.

On day two, the story of the Austin hit the front pages, calls flooded in from newspaper readers and we were overwhelmed with leads. The first came from photographer Mani Lama, who thought he'd photographed the car a few years before and brought in some images for us to see. A quick glance and Dad knew it wasn't the one.

Then we went to visit Kendra Bikram Shah, who owns several classic cars and reckoned he knew a man who might know where the Austin ended up. It was a pleasure to spend time with Kendra, who is as enthusiastic about cars as anyone I've met. Ken called an old mechanic of his, who had been working on cars in the valley for decades. The old guy remembered seeing the Austin, even

'We never seriously thought we'd find the car, but we also didn't expect such an enthusiastic response from the Nepalese'

remembered its license plate, but hadn't worked on it in the last 15 or 20 years. Then we had a phone call from the man from the Nepalese parliament who bought the car in 1964: he told us that he'd sold it a few years later, but couldn't remember or trace the person who'd bought it. We never seriously thought we'd find the car, but we also didn't expect such an enthusiastic response from the people of Kathmandu. Our visit struck a chord with car enthusiasts all over the city, and there's a chance it'll turn up one day.

The welcome our party received in Nepal will live with me forever. We were treated like royalty, not only by vintage car enthusiasts across the city, but even by the army, who showed us its collection of cars.

By the time we flew out of Kathmandu, five days after setting off from Delhi, we were all shattered. Dad and Bob had mixed feelings – it was exciting to return, but the place was shockingly different to how they remembered it, especially India. Ten times the number of people, a thousand times more traffic on the roads. It was blind luck that we got through it unscathed. Nepal was a joy. But I'd seen the mountains my father had been telling me about since I could understand speech, and that was worth the effort.

'It's the roof of the world, Bill,' he murmured, and I remembered him saying that to me years ago. Where would we be without dads, eh? Nowhere, that's where.

Just another near-death experience on the highways of India

Chapter 3

Aston Martin goes to Italy

The Aston Martin DB9 is a powerful yet understated car, a quintessential example of the best of British motoring . So how would it be greeted by the Italians?

Words Michael Harvey   Photography by James Bareham

THEY SAY 'ASTONE MARTIN' AND 'ASTON MARTEEN' BUT they know exactly who this stranger is; old men in shiny Sunday best, wearing suede shoes and felt hats, taking the long way home from Mass, stopping here for a coffee, there for a cigarette, and everywhere for a chat.

This morning, the truly devoted had been up before the swallows, gathered in small groups in the presence of their icons to pay homage to their disciples. Saint Michael had duly delivered. Saint Rubens, meanwhile, made an unfortunate choice of tyre compound, slid wide in the first session and never strung a decent set of laps together.

You can't escape Ferrari around here. His sign, the sign of the horse, is in every bar you visit. And every bar was still showing reruns of the Sepang communion. But then again, you can't escape cars around here.

All Italians feel intrinsically well disposed towards automobiles. Thanks to Ferrari, F1 is a national sport in Italy, taking as many headlines in the daily *Gazzetta dello Sport* as football. But these people, these old men who seemed to have unknowingly morphed into Enzo Ferrari clones (the hats, the waistcoats, the sunglasses...), these folks of Emilia-Romagna really understand cars.

If you wanted to know if this new Aston Martin could really cut it, could deliver up the potential of its engineering, could deliver on the promise of all those amazingly positive reviews; if it could breeze into the most venerated club in the world without so much as a nod to the doorman, then a weekend here, in and around Modena, would tell you everything.

Which is why, having collected the keys to our blue-grey DB9, in Nice of all places (I know, I know, I am a very lucky man), I found myself heading east towards Monaco and then beyond Ventimiglia into northern Italy, destination Portofino. Well, where else would you take what must be one of, if not the, most beautiful modern cars there is?

ITA

ASTON MARTIN IN ITALY

Vehicle: Aston Martin DB9
Climate: Competitive
Distance: 386 miles
Duration: 3 days and nights
Road Surface: Tarmac
Roadkill Roulette: Ferrari staff
Notes:
Get the Aston Martin DB9 into enemy
territory to see what they make of
it. Oh, and maybe race any other
supercars we see on the way.

The DB9 muscles in on Ferrari's territory. Quite successfully

A couple of Ferrari employees do their best to ignore the Aston

Henrik Fisker, the deeply charming and suspiciously well-tanned Dane who has steered Aston Martin design for the last two years, is on hand to wave goodbye as I steer what feels like a very big car through the narrow streets of Vence and Villeneuve-Loubet towards the autoroute. Fisker can claim all credit for the breathtakingly divergent interior that currently surrounds me.

He can take a lot of the credit for the exterior, but not all, since the original theme for the car was developed by Ian Callum, who gave us the DB7 and the Vanquish, and who began work on the DB9. These days, the Scot is charged with finding a similarly convincing design direction for Jaguar. Poor boy. That one is going to be tricky.

The DB9 doesn't have the presence of a Vanquish, but that's almost certainly part of a deliberate policy. After all, it costs close to £60,000 less, and with a different set of cogs would eclipse it in terms of performance; the DB9 packing 13bhp per tonne more than the identically-engined, six-litre V12 Vanquish. What it does have is an elegant, effortless, mature beauty that makes the once elegant, effortless and maturely beautiful DB7 now look ever so slightly gawky.

'It goes without saying that the DB9 is a wonderful tourer. And it's way too beautiful for the trash 'n' flash South of France'

The DB9 is way too beautiful for the south of France, where the trash 'n' flash Footballers' Wives aesthetic takes hold more strongly with every passing summer. Still, tomorrow morning we'll wake up in Portofino.

It goes without saying that the DB9 is a wonderful tourer, and especially at night when the bright illumination of the slightly Seventies looking instruments and the high-end, hi-fi-influenced centre console is comforting and kinda sexy. You learn pretty quickly that the best way to drive this six-speed auto is to use the little paddles (right up, left down) behind the steering wheel. Press the D button to the right of the row of PRND buttons midway up the dash (there are no sticks of any sort in this Aston, although a conventional six-speed manual will be available), and the familiar, traditional ZF six-speed auto transmission, complete with torque converter, starts to do its thing.

And rather makes a mess of it, to be frank, hunting up and down the ratios and generally being an irritant. Click it manually into sixth or fifth, however, and it will stay there and let the engine do the work. There is 420lb ft of torque down there, after all.

With the Vanquish, Aston succeeded in making automatic control of a manual gearbox work. With the DB9, it has succeeded in making manual control of an automatic work. It's a brilliant system – the little legend on the instruments tells me it's called Touchtronic 2.

Upchanges are quick and smooth. Downshifts similarly impressive – it even blips the engine if you time it right. Not bad for a slushmatic, eh?

But then this is a clever car: innovative, pragmatic, highly engineered. Grabbing a quick espresso and a sweet bun down by the harbour at Portofino while

Beautifully styled
and potently fast,
just like a certain
Mr James Bond

DB9

the rain gently spritzes the DB9's slim curves, it's impossible to imagine that this is a car which begins with a hydro-formed aluminium-intensive tub, a concept pioneered by Lotus and – literally – highly visible in the Elise.

Undressed, the DB9 is impressive and engineers might even call it elegant (it will, with a few tweaks here and there, form the basis for next year's Aston Martin Vantage, the V8-engine 911 alternative), but you and I might call it a mess. Hydro-forming – bending aluminium bits under extremely high water pressure – doesn't require the expense of investing in million-dollar machinery and so made the DB9 economically possible; but it does call for a barrowload of structurally efficient elements all glued and meshed together. Effective, but it ain't romantic. Unlike Portofino at this time of the year, at this time of the morning.

I love any part of the Riviera out of season, but Portofino at dawn, with the local shellfisher men heading out to pull their traps, is pretty much matchless for romance. And there, sat on the edge of the sea, is what is beginning, to me, to feel like the best grand tourer in the world.

Maybe the best car in the world.

> **'Portofino at dawn, with the local shellfisher men heading out to pull their traps, is pretty much matchless for romance'**

And we all know that when it comes to romance, there's nothing quite like a GT with a bloody great big engine up front. So it's time to leave Portofino behind, head back up the autostrada to Genoa, then inland to where we hope the roads will dry a little. And we might find ourselves something beautiful, Italian and big-engined to compare ourselves with.

And how we do. We first spot the Murcilago about one mile up the road, but it's bloody obvious what it is even before we move into audible range. As it is, we begin to hear the Lambo blowing just about when its driver sees us. You can guess what happens next. On a Saturday morning, on a sunny, dry empty autostrada, the Lambo and the Aston briefly get close to their top speeds, the Lambo not pulling away from the Aston by the time its driver thinks better of the situation at close to 170mph.

Aston Martin reckons the DB9 will sail all the way to 186mph. I reckon that's modest. Battle drawn, Dominic, the Lamborghini driver, complete with natty orange leather baseball jacket that matches his car's interior and exterior, suggests we pull the cars over and have a coffee.

It's very easy to forget just how effortlessly Lamborghini has held the monopoly on automotive theatre these past three decades. Closely following an orange Murciélago off the gas and onto the twisting slip roads of a service station, that enormous engine blowing and popping its way to a standstill, only for the driver's door to scissor up and the pilot to emerge, apparently metres in front of the midmounted engine, you can't help but feel a little inadequate in an Aston Martin, even if it has just proven in some small way that it's a match for the most badass supercar money can buy.

And (rather gratifying, this) the crowd these two cars draw is every bit as

interested in the DB9 as they are in the blood-orange bull. For the first time this weekend, I hear a familiar refrain, 'Preeeety car, preeeeety car.' Words you'll recall Rossano Brazzi uttered in *The Italian Job*, seconds before calling in the JCB to destroy Michael Caine's DB5 Volante.

Dominic, who sells gemstones, is on his third Lambo. The extraordinary noise it makes is the result of a non-standard exhaust he's had fitted.

He's only had it for a week and it's still tight.

It's no wonder, he reckons, that we were able to keep pace with him.

Well, maybe, but don't underestimate how quick the Aston is. Weighing in at just over 1,700kgs, thanks to that aluminium structure, and packing 450bhp, the DB9 is proper supercar quick. Even if, thanks to that gearbox, it doesn't always feel it. Scrap that, it's not just the ZF auto that takes the raw edge off this car, it's the sheer quality of its construction and the sheer elegance of that interior. Car stylists have banged on for years about the influence of modern furniture designers on their work, only for their interiors to look like, er, car interiors. Not this one.

Under the clear skies and in the morning sunlight which has now replaced the low cloud of the rainfiltered dawn, the DB9's interior is a wonderful place to be.

'Time to see what the boys at the Ferrari factory make of it. Very little, to be honest. The cult of Ferrari is far too pervasive'

Best of all, it feels like an Aston. I've read that some folks don't like the size and sweep of the dash, or the weight of the steering, but I reckon that's what makes it feel like an Aston. And it's not as if the car doesn't have uncharacteristically quick reflexes and can be driven like a racing GT. Astons have long trodden a line between supercar and muscle car, and this one is no different. And thank God for that. This might be the first Aston that goes like a Lambo and is built like a Porsche, but it still feels like an Aston Martin.

Time now to muscle down to Maranello and see what the boys coming off shift at the Ferrari factory make of it.

And what do they make of it? Very little, to be honest. They file out of the factory towards the car park. Some pause, stop and take a closer look. But the cult of Ferrari is far too pervasive.

It would have been disappointing had we left then and there. I've always wanted to watch a Grand Prix at the Ferrari Club Maranello, and we'd heard there was a classic Italian car rally in nearby Castelfranco Emilia, too. The reaction couldn't have been more different. At the Club, president Alberto Beccari welcomed us thus: 'A welcome to Maranello to you and your beautiful car.' What's more, when we turned up outside Castelfranco and asked, in poor Italian, if we might be admitted to the event, the caribiniere got on his radio and called up a motorcycle escort to take us right to the heart of the party.

Chilling out at one of Italy's many cafes. Mine's an espresso

Some of Italy's older boys offer their approval

USA

MUSTANG ACROSS USA

Vehicle: Ford Mustang
Climate: Sleazy and paranoid
Distance: 275 miles
Duration: 4 breakneck hours
Road Surface: Tarmac
Roadkill Roulette: None... could have been a different story if the best man had won...
Notes:
Welcome to the new Wild West – Ford Mustang versus aeroplane in a cross-desert race from LA to Vegas.

STOP

Chapter 4

Chasing the American dream

Whether it's the wagon trains rolling west or the beat generation bumming rides, America's mythology is built around the open road. Get your motor running...

Words Pat Devereux Photography by Anton Watts

IT'S TIME TO MAKE A GAMBLE. I'VE BEEN GRINDING OUT of LA in solid traffic for the last 30 miles on Interstate 10, tempers and temperatures rising all around me, precious time burning up and blowing away, and now I've come to a point in the journey that could make this weekend or destroy it completely. I've got to be in Vegas in four hours to meet The Girlfriend off her flight or I'll lose the $1,000 bet. I get a three-hour headstart in the car, she takes the plane. Last one there's a loser…

But do I turn off onto Interstate 15 and crawl all the way to Sin City on the back of this giant lava flow of cars and trucks? It's the obvious route to take – it's the most direct and has plenty of fuel stops. And I'll probably get there with half an hour to spare. Or should I keep going on the 10 for a while longer and then take a long cut I know, the one with no petrol stations, and no traffic? It'll be a tight squeeze but, if I don't get stopped, I think I can make it.

I look down at the Mustang's petrol gauge and it's still reading three-quarters full. I'm about 400yds from the exit for the 15 so I've only got a few seconds to make up my mind, but I don't need more than a fraction of the first one; I've decided already. If I'd been in an SUV or luxury barge with a suitably huge stereo and a fully loaded iPod, I might have just knocked my brain into neutral and followed the crowd. But in a manual V8 Mustang? Well, it was always going to be the long way round…

'It's a chunky car bashed out of steel for a blue collar audience. If Bruce Springsteen were a car he'd be a Ford Mustang GT'

The idea of driving to Vegas from Los Angeles might not seem like a brilliant idea at first. There are planes leaving at 15-minute intervals all day and some of the night from LAX to John Wayne Airport, just off the strip, that take a little under 45 minutes each way and cost less than a tank of fuel. You don't actually fly horizontally for more than a couple of minutes in most of them because as soon as you've taken off, you are preparing for landing. People who live in LA fly out for dinner in Vegas and fly home the same night. It's that close.

Plus there's the horrible traffic to take into account. Leave at the wrong time of day – like any day after 3pm or after midday on Friday and you'll spend the next six, or maybe seven, hours staring at the back of the car in front getting all existential. (The car is the symbol of freedom yet you've never felt more constricted in your life. Discuss.) And then bored, and then angry, and then tired, and then stoic, and then, just as you're about to get suicidal, you arrive.

But that's using the freeways. The route I'm heading to now couldn't be more different. It's actually the well-trodden route of the Rat Packers, who used the winding road to sashay between their homes in Palm Springs and their gigs in Vegas. It still requires you to spend some thinking time on the 10 freeway from LA to access it but, once you're on it, there's very little to take your mind off going as fast as possible.

Which is exactly the kind of road you want to be driving a modern V8 Mustang on. The styling might have been inspired by the classic 68 Mustang, but the handling is a lot less sloppy than it used to be. In the original car – I know; I own one – you need a rosary and change of underwear to get

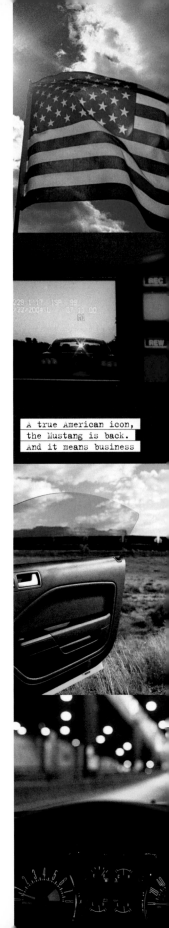

A true American icon, the Mustang is back. And it means business

Just like Mustangs from the past, the new version is no stranger to the petrol pump

Who wouldn't be tempted by the cultural gems on offer in Las Vegas?

through a series of bends quickly. In the latest 'Stang, as long as you don't over-drive it, you can get where you want to go fast.

It requires a very deliberate, almost old-fashioned style of input. It's best to take a slow in, fast out approach, getting all your braking done in a straight line, then giving it loads – and I mean loads – of throttle on the way out. The gearbox is a big, butch number that requires a man-sized shove in the right direction. But, once you get used to its unhurried action, you can row the car along surprisingly smoothly.

The way the car rides is nothing much to write home about, but the grip on offer is reassuring. However carefully you set up for corners, there's always one that tightens up unexpectedly, so it's good to know there's a margin for driver error built into the handling. True, it's not a terribly big margin, but it's there.

I think it's the analogue feel that is at the heart of the appeal of Ford's pony car. In a world of digital everything, it's a pleasure to get behind the wheel of something as basic as this. There are no swiveling head-lights, turbos, or anything (other than that odd instrument backlight col-our changer) that doesn't need to really be there. It's a big 5.4-litre V8 in a chunky car with chunky controls bashed out of steel for a blue collar audience that has matured well. If Bruce Springsteen were a car, he'd be a Ford Mustang GT.

> **'Seeing the yellow 'Stang launching over the hill towards him, I can see the cop's eyes widen even behind his shades'**

And perhaps The Boss's music should be included with every Mustang sold as it's making a lot of sense as the soundtrack to the film being played across the Ford's windscreen right now. I've just left the freeway behind and I'm haring up a winding hill into the mountains towards Twenty Nine Palms to begin the fun part of the journey. As the engine fills its lungs with premium unleaded, the exhaust note hardens and Bruce launches into *Born to Run* it's all good.

Or it is until I glance down at my watch and see that I've got less than three hours to get to Vegas airport. I think about calling The Girlfriend to check if she's been delayed, but then I look at my phone and it hasn't got any service. That's that then. My right foot reflexively sinks a little low-er on the throttle and my gaze moves a hundred yards further ahead. It's going to be an even faster drive than I thought…

At times like these my head immediately becomes a trip computer. My eyes flick between the odometer, the clock, the speedo and the horizon, working out what average speed I need to do to arrive on time. My arms and feet are linked subconsciously to the whole process so that the car's speed adjusts to whatever number my grey matter deems necessary to arrive on time. It's like active cruise control with no speed limiter.

Which is my way of saying that I didn't mean to be going quite so fast when I saw the top of the cop car's aerial appearing over the crest of the hill in front of me. I'd been going well up to this point, flashing past Roy's Diner on the old Route 66, the organic calculator figuring I would still be on time. But I felt the yellow Mustang and I could have been travelling a little faster than the limit. So I instinctively hit the brakes.

Maybe not quite hard enough…. Seeing the yellow 'Stang launching over the hill towards him, I can see the cop's eyes widen even behind his shades. I come off the brakes and let the engine slow us down, looking in the rear view mirror for the inevitable flashing blue and red lights. But, miracle of miracles, as I disappear down the hill nothing follows me.

I dawdle along for a mile or so, but all I can see is heat haze and all I can hear is the V8's exhaust note bouncing off the red rocks either side of me. Out here in Nowhere, CA, the cop must have thought he imagined it. Nothing, nothing, nothing, flying yellow Mustang, nothing, nothing, nothing. Can see his point, no?

Powering back up to a proper gallop, it's my turn to start seeing things. Up ahead in the distance is what looks like a massive rollercoaster growing out of the desert. I look away then look back and instead of being gone, it's got bigger. And it continues to get bigger until I realize that it is indeed a massive rollercoaster. My first thoughts are that I've taken a brilliant wrong turn and I'm almost in Vegas. But those hopes are dashed when I see a sign saying 'Welcome to Pahrump'. Pahrump indeed.

It's not all bad though as I'm back on the freeway now and still making good time. The sign says I've still got about 60 miles to run, with just under an hour to do it in, so I'm not too worried. A 60mph average even on this choked-up road should be possible. Should be, if I had any bleedin' petrol left, which I've just noted I haven't…

> **'A 60mph average even on this choked-up road should be possible. Should be, if I had any bleedin' petrol left, which I haven't'**

You can probably imagine a longer string of expletives than I said at that moment, but it's doubtful they would be as heartfelt. There aren't any petrol stations between Pahrump and Vegas, so I have to drive 10 miles further, swing the 'Stang around and charge back for fuel.

Screeching into the filling station, I leap out of the car, swipe the credit card and insert the nozzle all in one smooth movement. The old guy opposite looks over at me squeezing the pump handle like a vice. 'Priddy car you got there, son,' he drawls. I smile a thin smile back, no time to talk. 'How fast a car like that can go, huh?' 150, I say. 'Hew, how do you know that son?' I don't, I say, but if it doesn't I'm dead.

The next 30 minutes pass in a lurid frenzy of under- and over-taking that owes more to the Whacky Races than Le Mans, but now I can see the airport – it's closer than I thought – and I've still got three, maybe four, minutes left. Or not. Just as I think I'm going to make it, my mobile rings and it's her. The plane's only arrived early – early! – and she's on the way to the exit now. 'You are outside, aren't you?' she says smugly. Yeah, I'm outside, I reply. Outside the airport, I mutter under my breath.

So I lose the bet by just over a minute but, you know, I'm not too disappointed. The Girlfriend's had a quick flight but I've had a truly great drive. She thinks she made the right choice taking the plane – I know I made the right choice taking the Mustang. And ᵒI've just thought of a truly Vegas way to get my money back.

'Double or quits on the way home?' I say as she opens the door. She thinks about it for a second then turns to me. 'Hell yeah!'

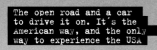

The open road and a car to drive it on. It's the American way, and the only way to experience the USA

‹NOR›

FERRARI IN NORWAY

Vehicle: Ferrari 430
Climate: Dark and clammy
Distance: 1254 miles
Duration: 4 days and 3 nights
Road Surface: Tarmac and potholes
Roadkill Roulette: One Ferrari tyre. Not very happy about that
Notes:
One of the last bastions of truly unspoilt road anywhere in the road, *Mad Max* scenery with 100-mile-long straights.

Chapter 5

Tunnel vision in Norway

If you want to hear just how good the engine of a Ferrari F430 sounds, take it to a tunnel. Actually, lots of them. And there's no better place for that than Norway

Words Tom Ford Photography by Lee Brimble

BANG... HISS...THRUMBLE... CRUMP. THE FRONT LEFT TYRE has just exploded on the Ferrari I'm driving. Which isn't the greatest feeling halfway up an almost entirely deserted Norwegian mountain. It's not that I'm super-sensitive or anything either – I can tell the tyre's decided to sigh its life away because the F430 has jerked sideways into the path of a battlefield-pocked yellow snowplough and my hands are still gripping tenaciously at quarter-to-three. My life has flashed before my eyes (colourful, but only time for highlights) and I've totally forgotten what to do. I decide to do nothing. The snowplough blares past, through the tightest of gaps and my passenger makes a face like someone has just kicked him very hard in the shins.

For some reason, my reaction to intense stress in wilderness/survival situations is to mentally count the food I have with me (eight cans of Red Bull, eight Jordans Crunch bars, a Jaffa Cake and six Mr Kipling Country Slices), but eventually I get it together long enough to bring us to a wobbly stop on the nearest snowy verge. We shudder to a rest outside the mountain tunnel through which we were passing, and a mixture of adrenalin and caffeine soon have me shaking like a drunk. We're OK. We're not dead. No worries.

I get out, take a look at where we are, wince, glance down at the three-inch hole in the sidewall of the shredded tyre, wince again, and commence swearing and stamping around like I'm being attacked by a swarm of invisible bees.

It doesn't really matter. The moment the car slewed away with its automotive clubfoot, the horrible realisation came that I'm by a tunnel halfway up a Norwegian mountain (but don't know which tunnel), I've just broken my (borrowed) £140k car, Norway doesn't have any Ferrari dealers, it's getting dark, it's minus four and I've forgotten my gloves. The mountain of ice behind us is creaking like a rusty bedstead and small bits keep falling off. Towards us.

I panic. There's a brief scuffle as the team tries to prevent me from creating an emergency Ray Mears-style bivouac from a stray piece of Armco and three sweaters, but eventually I calm down enough to take stock. I've promised Ferrari that the only UK press F430 Spider will come back without being stripped for parts by toothless Norwegians with crossbows, and we aren't even nearly safe, even if you mentally squint. The rest of the team seem more jolly, and keep taking snaps of the eye-strainingly beautiful views while standing with their hands on their hips and sighing like contentedly busted boilers.

The ferries come in useful when you run out of road

What every Ferrari owner should have; a mansion in the country

The roof of the Spyder has been down for a nice portion – except when horizontal rain decided to play hunt-the-gap-in-the-sweater – and sat in a little bubble of hot gas with the roof off and the heater up, it's like being on a safari for geologists. Obviously there's not as much tracking as if we were going for big game, but the sense of awe at the natural world is right up there. It looks like the mountains have been having a falling out and have knocked chunks out of each other. The sky is the colour of 10-day-old bruises, and even the trees are almost violently green against the greys and browns of the rock. But it's not depressing. Just crushingly majestic.

Perhaps I'd better explain. The idea behind this trip is that if you ever get yourself in a Ferrari Spyder of any description and you have any love of engines at all, the first thing you need to do is get yourself into an enclosed space, rev the nuts off it, and give yourself an eargasm. Obviously you can do this in your garage, but the disadvantage of choking to death on your own enjoyment can be a little too Michael Hutchence for my liking. Far better to find a tunnel and hit it when you can get a clear run between speed cameras. So we decided to go to the longest tunnel in the world – the Laerdal Tunnel in Norway.

'The sky is the colour of 10-day-old bruises, and even the trees are violently green. But it's not depressing, just majestic'

So we jumped aboard the ferry to Kristiansand for 18 hours, and motored through the icy backroads until we, er, broke the Ferrari. Now Ferrari is on the end of a very crackly phone line saying that it will 'see what it can do'. I really can't see anything those guys can do from an office in the UK, so proceed to panic a little more, just to keep warm.

After much back and forth and slightly whinnying descriptions of where we are and just how badly prepared we can possibly be (I didn't mention the Country Slices), we pump some 'get you home' gunk into the tyre and drive very slowly to the village of Roldahl, where we hunker down in a small shed in a caravan park because it's the only place we can find to stay this far out of season. Then we eat reindeer bolognese bought from the local petrol station and boiled to perfection by Lee, our photographer. We try not to look at each other, while wiping tyre sealant out of our hair.

Ferrari, in the best tradition, mounts a rescue mission. If you have access to some suitably stirring music (I found I was whistling *The Dam Busters March* in my head throughout the whole episode), this is the bit where you should be playing it at strenuous volume. Two engineers jump on a plane at an hour's notice, with a balanced wheel and tyre as hand luggage, and a tool bag in the hold. They fly to Bergen, hire a car and drive to the local ferry, which is shut.

The engine sits
like a work of art
behind glass

A slight risk
of going sideways
on these wet roads

'My ears explode, my brain caves in, the world just

warps - 4.3 litres of V8 seem to sense the occasion'

'Ferrari mounts a rescue mission. Two engineers jump on a plane with a balanced wheel and tyre as hand luggage, and a tool bag in the hold'

Eventually they get across the mighty fjord, and appear at our shed at 6am after travelling all night across a frozen mountain range in a Ford Focus and, bizarrely, they're smiling. Perhaps in relief at not dying in a budget rent-a-car somewhere unlocatable up a mountain. They are still wearing their official Ferrari coats and still manage to give me a ticking off for the state of the paint-work. Having changed the wheel in approximately three minutes, they attach a laptop, disengage any worrying warning lights from the dash, and leave. They were with us for 12 minutes. It's like being hit by the service crew version of the SAS. In. Sort it. Out.

They travelled 18 hours for that and it's unclear whether that would have happened if I had merely rung the AA. I'm left smoking a cigarette in a deserted caravan park on a Norwegian mountain with the vague sense that something utterly unreal just happened.

It has. But the Ferrari's fixed. And, after a few more phone calls, a few rough calculations and a few crossed fingers, it means we're still Laerdal Tunnel bound. I'm not sure I want to see any more tunnels. But it seems churlish to head home with our tails between legs after having come so far.

Getting there proves to be one of the world's great drives, if a little slower than I might have attempted had I not been worried about a second bout of stranding. The views just keep on mugging our senses with the experience equivalent of an iron bar. Norway out of season becomes something straight out of Grimm's. Big country. More spiky, dragon-dentistry mountains spearing skywards, jaws clamping hard on the sky. Nature with proper teeth and not emasculated by some development dork with a JCB and too little imagination.

The support car loses touch quickly, picking us up again as we realise that, when the tourists aren't here to witness it, the Norwegians break open the road-building manual and make repairs to every available surface. Not great for a 198mph supercar, having to pick its way through unmetalled roads full of ruts and troughs that even our Skoda Octavia 4x4 support car is troubled by.

We take a ferry to skip one bit of fjord, the boat appearing from the mist with its bow split asunder like that amazing sub-swallowing prop from the James Bond film. There are three cars on it. Two of them ours. It feels like we've stumbled across a country people are only just beginning to colonise. Somewhere harsh and beautiful, and weird as hell. Something legendary.

It takes another day and a bit to get to Aurland, near a town called Flåm (pronounced Flom), where the tunnel entrance begins. Too tired to go any further we check into a hotel that's surprised at the passing trade, and wait for nightfall. To avoid the traffic, I'm hitting the tunnel in the wee small hours.

In the intervening time, while I'm here in my hotel room with a hour to kill, I thought I'd do a little bit of explaining. The Laerdal Tunnel itself isn't just any old bit of pipe. This is an engineering marvel that bisects an entire mountain between Aurland and Laerdal, designed to connect Bergen and Oslo without the need to take ferries or climb over the top of a mountain pass in the middle of winter. It measures 24.5km. That's 15.2 miles. Which, to put it into perspective for modern petrolheads, is longer than a lap of the Nürburgring.

Getting twisted up through some awesome scenery

Time to put the roof up and get that heater going

The Norwegian landscape is like something out of the *Lord of the Rings*

Heading for another tunnel and another aural assault

That's one serious bit of amplifying tube, especially when your Ferrari has no roof. It certainly wakes you up. And also highlights the fact that I can't see any traffic in here, mainly because it's 3am and all the sensible people are tucked up in bed with the Norwegian equivalent of a Horlicks. We put the roof down in the first lay-by, and I'm struck by just how warm the tunnel is. I start to shake again. Excitement. Nerves. Then I pull gently out... and nail it.

My ears explode, my brain caves in, the world just warps. Four-point-three litres of V8 seem to sense the occasion, suck in a big lungful and spit it out as hard as they possibly can, ejecting a sonic wall straight out from the four tail pipes. My head snaps back into the headrest as the rev counter shrieks past 7,500rpm. A millisecond and 500rpm later I twitch my right hand and second gear hits home, bringing with it one of the most glorious noises ever to grace our planet. There's some petrol-powered epiphany that makes my eyes water and my senses melt.

In first, I was just holding on, to be blunt. Dealing with a little wheelspin, making sure things are OK. In second and third I sat back and appreciated the kind of fear that I imagine Neanderthal man got from going bare-knuckle with

'At 100mph, your ears pop. At 120mph the noise disappears. It feels like you've broken the sound barrier, or gone deaf'

a woolly mammoth. In a tunnel of this size and diameter, the noise has nowhere to go. It can't dissipate, or be absorbed by furniture, the rock just fires it straight back at you. I guess it must be something like big wave surfing. You get propelled by something monstrous just inches behind you – you can't see it, but my God, it's there. Boiling the air about a foot from your back bumper.

At 100mph, your ears pop. At 120mph you leave the noise behind. It feels like you've broken the sound barrier, or gone a bit deaf. All you've really done is breach the Ferrari's aerodynamics so that wind-roar takes over from exhaust bellow as the dominant sonic force – but it still feels eerily silent.

When we stop, I can't speak. All I can do is puff out my cheeks and blow air, shaking my head a little bit, wide-eyed. This does not happen often. Apparently, when Art Ed Norris heard us coming he broke out the video recorder to film us. Three or four minutes later, he was still waiting. He could hear the Ferrari for what must have been 6 or 7 miles. Imagine what it was like being sat inside it. If I'm honest, I can still hear it now. The noise is etched into the grooves of my brain like an old bit of vinyl.

At the end of the tunnel I turn around, look back down the gullet of the Laerdal and smile. Then I pull out, point the nose of the F430 into hell's gateway and... reprise.

Put your foot down,
sit back and soak
up the sounds

Not the best time
of year to be here.
But there's no traffic

AUS

< >

THE STUART HIGHWAY

Vehicle: Ford Falcon Typhoon mate
Climate: Bloody hot mate
Distance: 1,864 miles
Duration: 4 days and nights
Road Surface: Red, red earth
Roadkill Roulette: 2 possums, 1 skunk and a roo
Notes:
One of the last bastions of truly unspoilt road anywhere in the road, madmax scenery with 100-mile long straights. Ripper..

Daly Waters Pub
OUTBACK SERVO

FUEL
ASK AT THE PUB

DANGER
NO SMOKING
TURN OFF
ENGINE
BEFORE
OPENING
FUEL TANK

Chapter 6.

Where the wild things are

The Stuart Highway takes you into the Australian Outback and out of history, to a world dominated by the sun, the stars and red earth. Perfect for a Ford ute

Words Bill Thomas Photography by Mark Bramley

NORM MACLEAN LEANS FORWARD ON HIS BAR STOOL, ROLLS a cigarette and says: 'We know we don't usually travel at more than 130kmh, Clare, but who the hell are you to tell us that we can't?'

It's after 11pm, and if we aren't in the middle of nowhere right now, then we must be close. The crickets outside are loud and constant, and the road is quiet.

Norm is in charge here at Dunmarra Station, some 400 miles south of Darwin in the Northern Territory. I am three quarters of the way through a 1,864-mile journey from Adelaide to Darwin, straight up the centre of Australia from south to north along the Stuart Highway, and this is the last overnight stop before the final day.

So, we're starting in the middle, but this is a story that was always going to start in the middle. The middle is what it's all about. The Northern Territory is the desert state, where the sand is as red as the evening sky, and the milky way shines so brightly at night it almost hurts your eyes. Norm, a big-hearted, sharp-speaking, true-blue Ocker who traces his roots back to Stornaway, has lived in the Territory for many years – his ciggy now burning brightly, his eyes alive over a full goatee beard and a chin that could break bricks, MacLean warms to his theme:

'The people who live in the Territory are aware of the dangers. We drive to suit the conditions, so that means 130kmh is about as fast as we want to go, even in broad daylight. But turning us into criminals for going faster than that isn't right. The opposition party has made the speed limit an election issue, saying they'll abolish it again if they get into power, so it might be goodbye Clare.'

'Clare' is the Right Honourable Clare Martin, Chief Minister of the Northern Territory Government. It was her decision to slap a blanket speed limit of 110–130kmh (roughly 70–80mph) on the Stuart Highway, the first out-of-town speed limit in the Territory's 96-year history, and it's a decision that hasn't gone down well with Territorians. It smacks of revenue-raising and do-gooder political idiocy, the need to be seen to be doing something, while more expensive and complicated issues – driver training, driver awareness, driver fatigue, vehicle roadworthiness – are buried.

The same sort of thinking has turned the rest of Australia into a police state, with robotic draconian cops targeted to write as many speeding tickets as they can. No figures have been produced to prove the benefit of stricter speed limits in this country and it's likely they never will be, and while the debate rages on websites like no-speedlimit.com, Norm's take on it is clear enough.

'Territorians are easy-going people,' he says. 'But force them into a corner and they'll bite.'

The new Stuart Highway speed limit came into force on 1 January 2007 and it's been big news in Australia. Big enough for Holden, the country's arm of GM, to refuse to lend *Top Gear* a car for this journey. Holden, it would seem, saw it as 'one last run' for a couple of foreigners who would probably break the speed limit and crash. Despite my assurances that it was nothing of the sort, and despite stressing that photographer Bramley and I are Australian and understand the issues, Holden wouldn't budge. So, the slightly more switched-on people at Ford stepped up to the plate with an FPV F6 Tornado, a four-litre straight six, turbocharged, 360bhp Falcon ute, tuned by the boffins at Ford Performance Vehicles. Should get us there all right. Ripper, etcetera.

When we set off from Glenelg in Adelaide on the Southern Ocean coast, our nav read 34 hours 36 minutes and 1,879 miles to run to Darwin. No worries. The aim was Coober Pedy by the end of this first day, Alice Springs by the end of day two, via Uluru, a day of shooting in Alice and a bit of a rest, Dunmarra the next night, then a plane out of Darwin the day after, once we'd gazed out over the Timor Sea. Drives don't get more epic than this.

> '**When we set off from the Southern Ocean coast, our nav read 34 hours 36 minutes and 1,879 miles to Darwin. Drives don't get more epic than this**'

Look closely and you'll notice a very thin aerial stuck to the top of the Tornado's roof. This two-way radio is a key part of this story, and if you're thinking of driving the Stuart Highway, you should spend a few quid on a basic radio like this. It allows you to talk to Road Train drivers, and despite what you might think, these blokes want you to talk to them. Not because they're lonely, but because any sort of mishap involving a car holds them up. They, more than anyone, want people to understand how to drive this road properly and not get into trouble.

'Copy southbound,' said Bramley into the handset once we'd cleared the Adelaide area and got into open country. A big Road Train had just blown past in the opposite direction, the blast from its passing knocking the car sideways. The trucker was straight back to us.

'G'day mate,' he said.

'Anything happening up north?'

'Nah mate, nothing, just a few head of stray cattle a couple of clicks north of Glendambo. You go over a ridge then down through a couple of corners and they're near the second corner.' We chatted to him while he stayed in range, and he was like every trucker we spoke to over the next few days: friendly, well-spoken, bright and helpful. Every piece of advice we received was useful, sightings of cattle were accurate and the truckers were mildly surprised to be speaking to someone in a car.

Travelling in Australia is all about vast distances, of course, but you soon get into a rhythm. Adelaide to Cooper Pedy is 520 miles, so it's London to

Red earth, blue car and a world of Outback colour

If Skippy turns up now, you will be kissing your ute goodbye...

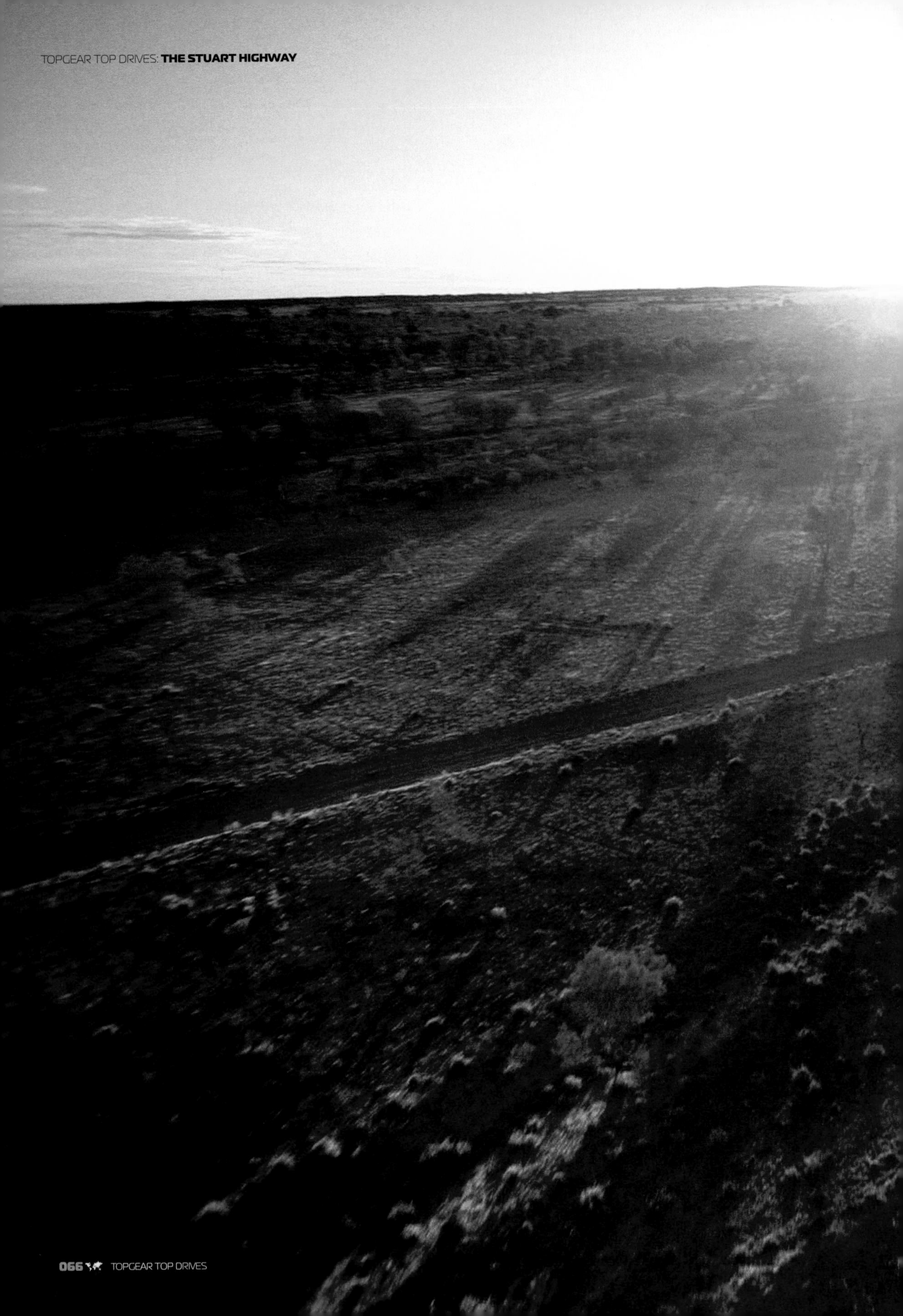

A chance to create
your own little
dust storm in the
vast wilderness

Best keep those
windows up driving
through this dust

Alice Springs
Pt Augusta

Dusk fast approaches
and the sky fills with
thousands of stars

ROAD TRAIN

Not the kind of place
you're likely to find
yourself stuck in traffic

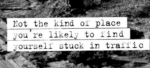

Darwin

PERTH

BARRON
CENTRAL COAST C
BRISBANE
CANBERRA

34:36 hrs - 3024 km
Fastest route

Route

Glasgow plus a hundred. Cooper Pedy is a beautiful, old, opal mining town with a classic Aussie main street. The outskirts are packed with clapped-out old mining rigs straight from Mad Max. Tough work, prospecting.

The first highway patrol copper we met was the only female one in South Australia. Constable Denise Case, a beautiful name for a police officer, pulled me over because she thought I had a radar detector, which are illegal in this state. No, I explained, I had braked from 90mph to 70mph because I'd seen her early and didn't want her to lock her radar on. We ended up talking for about half an hour, mostly about cars, and especially her's; a Commodore with a six-litre V8 engine. These are due to be replaced soon with V6-engined cars, and she wasn't happy about it. When we asked her to do a burnout for us in this, the last of the V8 interceptors, she said she'd love to. But, er, it'd be more than her job was worth. I've never seen a copper more keen to do something unlawful.

The South Australian leg of the trip passed without incident – though it's an epic journey in itself, it isn't until you reach the Northern Territory that you start to see the red dust and get a proper flavour of the Outback.

Best to let Mark Bramley's photographs tell the story of this magnificent country – my piffling scribbles can't hope to do them justice. The old indiginous bloke on the opposite page was on his way to a settlement about 500 miles away from Uluru. We destroyed an alloy wheel doing the high-speed dirt road shots with the helicopter, but boy, was it worth it. And then there was Uluru. Majestic Uluru, the red heart of Australia. We timed our arrival perfectly at sunset, and just stood and watched in awe as the sky darkened and the rock changed colour.

If the 24-hour flight is putting you off visiting Oz, get a grip, cobber. Buy some sleeping tablets, set a date – and be sure to visit this magical place. To stand and watch Uluru at sunset on a clear evening is one of the most moving experiences imaginable, particularly so for me, because, despite being an Aussie, I'd never seen it. Typical that the peace of the moment was wrecked by a couple of tourist helicopters, but that's progress.

Uluru was called Ayers Rock until recently, named after a chubby South Australian politician with a bad beard. Now it's part of the Uluru–Kata Tjuta National Park, and is run by the Yankunytjatjara and Pitjantjatjara landowners, commonly known as the Anangu. They urge you not to climb it, though it's not against the law.

'Climbing is not the real thing about this place. The real thing is listening to everything,' say the Anangu. In a scant hour here, I learned what the real Australia is all about. I will never call it Ayers Rock again.

That night, we slept in the open desert a hundred miles from Uluru and looked at the sky. No light pollution out here, of course, and when your eyes adjust, the stars are utterly jaw-dropping. It was a new moon, too, which made the Milky Way even more spectacular. A tip: look at the moon phases and make sure you get a darker sky.

As Bramley set up his six-hour exposure shot of the stars, I looked at the ute-shape silhouette of the F6. There's something charming about the way cars wait to do your bidding. There it was, ready to go again, to get us back to civilization. It is a fantastic car, like a big coupé, Aussie-style. Ford worldwide should fit this engine to more of its cars. The Tornado was smooth, quiet, quick, and never missed a beat, averaging 29mpg to boot.

And when that Tornado rolled into Dunmarra Station at night, its head-lights sprayed with a multi-coloured vomit of bugs that looked like an abstract work of art, Victorian plates on full display, Norm MacLean wasn't impressed. He didn't seem too impressed when he first saw us, and he told us later that he wasn't impressed. But at least we were staying – he cooked us a couple of superb steaks, then we got talking and found out more about the real Stuart Highway and how to approach it.

The thing is, he hates seeing people arrive at Dunmarra after nightfall, because he's worried about the risks they face out on the road. The cattle are bad, but the roos are the biggest menace – there are literally millions of them, all migrating in the cooler night-time atmosphere. To give myself even a slight chance of missing any high-speed roo that might enter the picture from stage left or right, I didn't dare travel at more than 40 to 50mph.

'Territorians very rarely drive after dark. If you see a car at night, nearly always it won't have Territory plates on it. It'll be New South Wales, Victorian or Queensland plates, out-of-state people who don't know what they're doing. The trucks are different – roos bounce off them.'

When he mentioned that, I remembered talking to one trucker who said that he'd hit a roo that was big enough to make his truck shudder. A 50-metre

> **'Norm worries about the risks people face out on the road after nightfall. The cattle are bad, and the roos are a massive menace'**

long, 12-tonne vehicle actually shuddered. What that would have done to a normal car doesn't bear thinking about.

'Two young couples stopped in here the other night, late, about 11pm,' says Norm. 'They were in an old Toyota Tarago van. No bullbar, no spotlights. I asked them how much water they had on board, and they held up a couple of 500ml bottles. Incredible.'

Just as he finishes this sentence, a car pulls up to the petrol pumps – a Holden rental. We can see from inside the station that the plates are from NSW, and Norm gives me a knowing look before walking to the tills. It's a family, two adults and two young children, travelling in the depths of night without a care in the world. The bloke's wearing shorts and sandals and he smacks at a mosquito on his leg as he fills the tank. Norm has a quiet word with him, trying to convince him to stay, but no, the fool carries on. We didn't hear any word of a prang from the truckers the next morning, so by blind luck, they made it through unhurt.

Norm and I talk about the road for a while longer – about Falconio, the Overland Telegraph Line and The Ghan Railway, which shadows the Stuart Highway for most of its length. MacLean knows about the history of this place and tells a great story. Most of all, he hopes his message gets through: be safe. Sure, it'd be better without the speed limit, but even at 80mph, the Stuart Highway is still the greatest road on earth. Treat it with care.

IN MEMORY OF
KEITH (SLIM) ALAN PRITCHARD
TIMOTHY LINKLATER OFFICIAL
AKIHIRO KABE COMPETITOR
TAKESHI OKANO COMPETITOR
WHO DIED AT THIS LOCATION AS A RESULT
TRAGIC ACCIDENT, DURING THE
INAUGURAL NORTHERN TERRITORY
CANNONBALL RUN ON:
TUESDAY 24 MAY 1994.
'THEY DIED PARTICIPATING
THE SPORT THEY LOVED'

Dehydrated

Bullshi

FOR THOSE WHO ARE FULL O
Just add water

Arriving at the tropical north coast. Time to take that dingy from the back

NO
worries

Make sure you pack plenty of food and water. And a reliable phone. It's pretty remote in the Outback

< ARC >

SMART IN LAPLAND

Vehicle: Smart Fortwo
Climate: Furry
Distance: 598 miles
Duration: 4 days and nights
Road Surface: Well-pawed
Roadkill Roulette: A few elves had their reactions tested...
Notes:
Driving a Smart in a Finnish winter might seem a bit barmy, but with dog power as back-up, we're heading for the Northern Lights.

Chapter 7

Not a Smart thing to do

Lapland in northern Scandinavia is famous for a certain resident that wears red, but not this one. Still, it's about the right size for Santa's little helpers

Words Alistair Weaver Photography by Tom Salt

'A typical temperature in early spring is a "comfortable" -20 Celsius. Anything below -30 is "cold". The heater is working overtime'

THE SMART'S THERMOMETER reads -30 degrees Celsius as we leave Rovaniemi. The road ahead is clear and the buzz of the heater blends with the gentle throb of the tiny 698cc engine, while the studded tyres do battle with roads that could double as an ice rink.

To the scattered audience of moose, reindeer and huskies, we must be an extraordinary sight. A lanky Englishman is spearing across the Arctic in an odd red igloo, leaving behind the Lapp capital and the last remnants of civilization.

Inside our tiny capsule, photographer Tom and I are feeling cosy. The heater is just about keeping us warm, my iPod is set to 'easy listening', and we've a ready supply of reindeer salami. We might be a thousand miles from the Smart's natural, metropolitan habitat, but DaimlerChrysler's problem child has always felt strangely at home on the open road.

Ever since I drove Sir Stirling Moss's personal import in '98, I've been a fan of the Smart. It was a brand that was trying to offer something genuinely different in an over-congested market

and, while the execution was flawed, it had great charm. Which other modern car is worthy of a place in New York's Museum of Modern Art?

The Smart we've got is standard, save for snow tyres and an electric plug socket, which must be connected to the mains at night to keep the car functioning in temperatures that could dip as low as -50 Celsius. A typical temperature in early spring is a 'comfortable' -20, but anything below -30 is 'genuinely cold'. In such conditions, the little heater has to work overtime.

One of the local
means of transport.
And cute with it

A quick check of
the studded snow
tyres. Yep, all good

Reindeer are essential to life in this remote part of northern Europe

Nature's celebrated light show starts right on cue

work and our 'survival gear' consists of a down-filled jumpsuit.

Eventually, the road reveals a wooden hut, several reindeer and a bloke in a garish costume. At a guess, I'd say Eric Hatta is 50 years old. He has the wise, weathered face of a man who's spent his life outdoors. He's dressed in traditional Sami garb, with a garish jumper, reindeer-skin trousers and sieparat shoes. These boast upturned toes, like pixie boots, which can be bound to create makeshift skis. The outfit is a sop to the tourists, but it's also worn during Sami festivals.

For the past 10 years, Hatta and Kamu – his reindeer – have been employed in the tourist trade, but his background reads like a Monty Python sketch. 'My family has been reindeer herders for hundreds of years,' he explains. 'My grandfather, father and brothers are all herders.'

The farm is tantalisingly close to the Russian border. All the guide books tell us it will take at least a couple of weeks to gather the requisite paper-work, but in the spirit of adventure, we decide to make a run for it. At sunset and much to the amusement of the Finnish border guards, a tiny red capsule arrives at the border post.

The Finnish border post is a few hundred metres in front of the Russian equivalent, in between which is a no-man's-land. Feeling a bit like Steve McQueen, I peer out into the gloom and just catch sight of the opposing camp. 'We cross some-times,' says a friendly Finnish guard. 'The fuel's cheaper over there.' They pose for pictures with the Smart before turning us around.

After our near-Russian adventure, the hotel in Inari feels like a bit of an anti-climax. Dinner consists, as you might expect, of reindeer. But don't knock it. Up here, they provide food, clothing and income. Good reindeer

PRU

FERRARI IN THE ANDES

Vehicle: Ferrari 599 GTB
Climate: Bloody hot mate
Distance: 1,657 miles
Duration: 10 days and nights
Road Surface: Rocky
Roadkill Roulette: One backside, owing to tough suspension
Notes:
Taking a Ferrari over the Andes provokes the kind of surprise in the locals we feel attempting it. Will we make it from Peru to Ecquador?

Chapter 8

Taking on the impossible

Drive a Ferrari 599 across the Andes? Surely it's a trip that puts this car way out of its depth. But then, from these majestic heights, anything looks possible

Words Tom Ford Photography by Lee Brimble

¡HOLA ECUADOR!

V-Power

www.ferrariworld.com

Even the kids stand taller than the Ferrari 599

side of a mountain with little thought for either health or safety, you wouldn't expect traffic volumes to be heavy. Too many precipitous tonnes of rocks to fall on your head for one thing.

To the right is a 1,000-foot, near vertical drop into an undoubtedly uncomfortable mangled-up death on the jagged rocks of the valley floor; to the left a sheer rock face that offers no comfort, or even much scope for a panicky last scrabble for salvation. The next 90 miles of our journey will involve only car-crippling off-road driving, and even though this knife-in-the-back countryside would provide an excellent test for something like a Range Rover

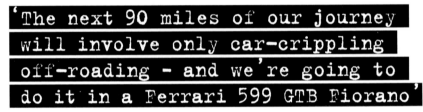

'The next 90 miles of our journey will involve only car-crippling off-roading – and we're going to do it in a Ferrari 599 GTB Fiorano'

ONE MINUTE THE VIEW IS OF the greens and browns of a countryside filleted and spatchcocked across the horizon, viewed from a 4,500m vantage point that quite literally takes your breath away. The next, that horizon is mugged by the greedy little rocky fingers of a gorge that rises up out of nowhere, gobbling up the forward view in a series of tunnels and crevasses that leave nothing but a streak of sky in a 150ft-wide slash above the car. As we enter the Andes proper, here in darkest Peru, the sounds start to reflect back on themselves and change – and so does the mood.

The Ferrari we are driving starts to feel both very small and nowhere near tall enough. Looking on the bright side, at least traffic is light. Of course, when the road has turned into a ledge with delusions of grandeur, seven feet of rock-strewn shelf carved into the

– ride height and four-by-four traction being the real winners – we're going to do it in a Ferrari 599 GTB Fiorano.

I know, I know. That last bit sounds like a joke, right? Well, no. As part of its Panamerica 20,000 challenge, Ferrari is taking two 599s from the tail to the top of the Americas, and our leg traverses the spectacular terrain of the Andes. If driving the 599 is an event in itself, then doing so the length of Peru and into Ecuador must rate highly on the list of things to do. Personally, I'm having trouble concentrating. The main reason being that I'm less concerned about the dodgy road, than the Ferrari's ability to actually get to the other end without being eviscerated by a piece of Peruvian rock.

It doesn't help that the noises the underside of the Ferrari is making are wincingly uncomfortable, the kind of noises that signify expensive repairs

ANTES·DE INGRESAR·AL TUNEL TOQUE·CLAXON

Agip
Lubricantes

FOR EXP
FOR EXT

The blessed relief
of some genuinely
smooth tarmac

Bienvenidos a Ecuador
Welcome to Ecuador   Ecuador

CUIDADO
ZONA DE
NEBLINA

'To the right is a 1,000-foot, near vertical drop into an undoubtedly uncomfortable mangled-up death on the jagged rocks of the valley floor'

The breathtaking panorama as the 599 cuts through the Andes

involving skilled welding. Every bump elicits hissing intakes of breath from both photographer Lee and me, but there's very little I can do to avoid the suspension GBH. There's not much room for manoeuvre. I've been trying to ride the tops or sides of the ruts and save the belly of the car, but that brings the fat bottom of the 599 perilously close to the edge of the drop – of which I'm acutely aware, thanks to Lee's indrawn breath and tendency to lean left when he thinks the edge is looming too large.

Thankfully, the 599 had been given a touch of toughening up by Ferrari in preparation for this trip, otherwise we'd still be in Lima with four flat tyres and a Ferrari in kit form. Also, and I may have neglected to mention

highway sections, traffic laws are somewhat optional, given that I have already been overtaken by several coaches doing 75mph on what amounts to a hopelessly maintained B-road back home. People are hanging from the roofs nonchalantly waving, which is a bit disconcerting.

Such overtaking humiliation wouldn't usually have occurred, except that at the time I was trying to avoid ripping the suspension off the Ferrari in one of the randomly regular open-cast mines masquerading as pot-holes in these parts.

Wherever we pause, a huge crowd gathers to gawp. Though the crowds are bigger in the larger towns like Trujillo and Huarez, the real delight comes from small mountain villages

'So far it's not been an easy ride, and I'm having no trouble figuring out why Paddington Bear left in search of better marmalade'

this fact to make myself sound a little more heroic, we're not actually on our own. Ferrari has sent a small army of employees along to accompany its pair of 599s on their 20,000-mile route around South America from Bela Horizonte in Argentina and up into the US and Canada, before a big party in New York three months later. It's an ambitious trip, for which we've joined them for the longest, most bizarre leg – the Peruvian Andes into Ecuador. Lima to Quito.

So far it's not been an easy ride, and I'm having no trouble figuring out why Paddington Bear emigrated in search of better marmalade. Driving through Peru is like playing Russian roulette with an Uzi – guaranteed to end in a sticky mess that nobody really wants to clear up. On the

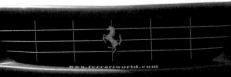

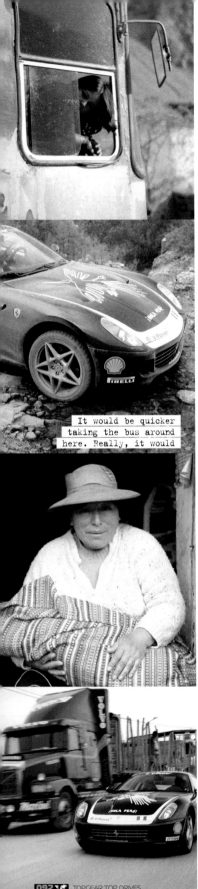

It would be quicker taking the bus around here. Really, it would

that see little more than the occasional care-worn 4x4, let alone 200mph Ferraris. A couple of times, I thought we were literally dropping off the map, only to round a corner and find a village having a festival complete with mariachi band at full volume.

Diminutive, nut-brown women dressed in traditional bright ruffs and frills eyed the Ferraris with bemused surprise before trying to make us dance for their amusement and bet on the donkey race that had closed the road. Everywhere was the sense of joy and community that you don't get in the west because everyone is too concerned with getting on. There's also a sense of welcome for strangers, the innocent interest that gets strangled by suspicion pretty much everywhere else I've ever visited. Here, the local kids will come and laugh at your blondness. They prod you. They touch the Ferrari.

It's not the sort of place that the Ferrari can really dance across and leave little sign of its passing, either. Driving for hours in these conditions is gruelling both for the mind and body of the driver and the mechanicals of any car, let alone one with such focused performance potential. But every day the surroundings more than make up for it. Some mountains are so high they spit in the eye of anything Europe has to offer, topping out with roadways at over 4,500m. Up here, if you run around for a bit, the low oxygen levels mean that you'll feel like you're trying to heave a desperately needed lungful of air through a small straw. Hearts beat like kettledrums, racing to keep up with the demand for more oxygen from an atmosphere that isn't capable of providing it. The cars slow down too and feel as if their 620bhp had been reined in to more like 350–400bhp. If the car can't breathe, it can't do.

A simple but effective cure for the humans is the coca leaf. Wad 10 of these bitter-tasting, dried leaves up under your lip and suck on them for a bit, and the burgeoning altitude sickness dissipates with surprising speed. No such luck for the cars – despite some careful planning, the gas we've been feeding them could easily be alcohol. It even smells different at the pumps. Still, as long as the Ferrari is moving I'm happy, because the walk home would take a while.

Besides, being at this altitude has advantages, too. The scenery never ceases to draw you around the next corner. Some 125 miles to our right is the Amazon, yet we drive through deserts and mountains so spectacular that you can't imagine jungle anywhere nearby.

Highly political, hand-painted electioneering messages adorn every wall in every village. Vote for 'Allan' seems popular, but the party of 'Angel and Boris' becomes a blue Ferrari favourite all the way to the Ecuadorian border.

It takes us five days, but eventually we get to cleave our stylish little way into our country of destination... The border crossing itself is a flurry of paperwork, passport stamps and fuggy smells of livestock and low-quality fuel. Peru took us six days to traverse, each day very much the same, but no less impressive for that.

Eventually, we reach Quito, and the terminus of our trip. The Ferraris are continuing, and a few days in their company doesn't feel like enough. There's so much more here. More to see, more to experience. Being here in these cars just seems to highlight what there isn't, just as much as what there is. All we've had in the past 10 days is a glimpse of South America through the unfamiliar lens of a Ferrari windscreen. And it won't be forgotten in a hurry.

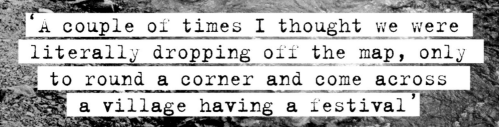

'A couple of times I thought we were literally dropping off the map, only to round a corner and come across a village having a festival'

MONDEO UP THE M1

Vehicle: Ford Mondeo
Climate: Thawing
Distance: 2,356 miles
Duration: 8 days and 7 nights
Road Surface: Dust, tarmac, the lot
Roadkill Roulette: Quite a lot of
cooked fish, some old tanks
Notes:
Driving through the former Eastern
Bloc countries might seem a bit
dangerous, but if you've got the
guns, why not give it a try, eh?

Chapter 9

To Russia with love

You'll know the M1 that runs the length of England, but
the M1 from Warsaw to Moscow? We took a
Ford Mondeo and headed off to the Wild East

Words Bill Thomas Photography by Alex P

'Guns? Jesus, all I wanted to do was drive a
Mondeo up the M1 from Warsaw to Moscow.
It's a road that's beckoned me for years'

DRAMA KICKED IN HARD THE instant this feature idea was aired – drama bordering on the hysterical. Anyone who'd heard any half-rumour about driving into the former Warsaw Pact countries had a word of warning.

'Bandit country' it is, apparently, 'like the Wild West, except East.' 'The border crossings are impossible.' 'You'll get hijacked if you take a car there – a Mondeo's worth five trillion times the average wage, so why wouldn't they steal it?' 'Some German tourists were shot last week.' 'Everyone carries an AK-47. Even children.' 'Journalists have been jailed in Minsk – and then executed by firing squad.' And so it went on in a similar vein, until editor Harvey chipped in: 'I have a friend in Moscow. He'll meet you at the Belarus border in a Discovery full of men with guns.'

Guns? Jesus, all I wanted to do was drive a Mondeo up the M1, from Warsaw to Moscow. It's a road that's beckoned me for years – 760 miles long, so a bit more substantial than the British M1's 193 miles, and a tad different, hopefully. It just needed a proper new Mondeo for a test. And here it is, bigger, sleeker and almost certainly better.

I rang the Russian consulate in London to tell them what I was planning and ask about visas.

'You should take the northern route through Lithuania,' said the thickly-accented Russian voice on the other end of the line. 'Do not drive through Belarus.'

'Why not?' I asked, interested now. If the Russian embassy was warning against it, maybe there was a hint of truth to the rumours.

The Eastern Bloc is emerging from the shadow of Communism

'Kolya advised us to bring a few US dollars in cash and some cigarettes to "talk" to the police. And he had his own guns'

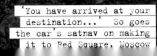

'You have arrived at your destination...' So goes the car's satnav on making it to Red Square, Moscow

'Because we do not know what the current situation is in Belarus – and neither do you.'

Oh. Good answer. I don't. A million warnings came flooding back into my head. But the plan couldn't change. The M1 runs from Brest on he border, all the way through Belarus, and it was the way I was going. What's more, I would dress up in a shirt and tie and try to look like a sales rep – and wear a pair of sunglasses that were a gift on the original Audi Quattro press launch in 1981, to boot.

'We do not know what the situation is in Belarus and neither do you.' Hmm. I rang Nikolay Kachurin ('Kolya', for short), the editor of *Top Gear* magazine in Russia, to ask what this meant exactly. I told him about the Lithuanian suggestion, and mentioned the editor's plan for a Discovery packed with armed men.

'No!' said Kolya. 'You will need none of this! It isn't bandit country, it will be safe. Besides, we have our own guns.'

Kolya's word was enough. He said he would meet us at the frontier and 'get us over'. He told us about the visas we'd need. He advised us to bring a few US dollars and some cigarettes to help 'talk' to the police. Nothing indicated any hint of doubt. And he had his own guns.

Expensive Belarussian and Russian journalist visas sorted, Kolya standing by with guns, brand new Mondeo 2.0-litre diesel ready to go – the only thing left to do was to hop on a plane to Warsaw and head for the Wild Wild East. The M1 doesn't officially start in Warsaw, but the road leading east from the Polish capital becomes the M1 when you get across the border. It's part of the European Route 30, which actually starts in Cork and winds all the way to Moscow.

The old people in this part of the world have seen a lot of change. But not a new Mondeo

Some guns, some issues of *Top Gear*; the essential items to pack on this trip

why there aren't more old Audi 100s on the road, wonder no more – they're in Belarus. We were waved straight to the front of this motley queue by friendly Polish border guards, who took our passports and documents away and checked them for a full hour. This is normal procedure for a new vehicle which hasn't crossed the border before, apparently – making sure it isn't nicked. It gave me plenty of time to admire the Polish checkpoint area, which consisted of a bunch of unpainted prefab metal boxes lined up like cargo containers under a big metal roof. The whole thing sat on a swamp near the river Bug. You can see past a bridge crossing the Bug to the Belarus checkpoint, which had a roof in a light blue colour, dominated by a single, huge, red and green Belarus flag fluttering from a tower.

Once released by the Polish guards,

As I attempted to leave the city and got lost in busy afternoon traffic, my first impressions of the Mondeo were very positive. It immediately felt well engineered, solid and refined, perfect for long-distance driving. The car also has tremendous boot and cabin space and, especially when in the softest of its three settings, it is a wonderfully supple, absorbent ride.

Then again, it needed to be on the road to Biala Podlaska, our overnight stop on the border – the E30 here is absolutely horrid. Endless roadworks and potholes and dreadful surface chop, and most of it on a three-lane road, so you're constantly battling at high speed against oncoming traffic in the central overtaking lane. Biala Podlaska is a pretty nondescript town about the size of Scunthorpe. Only complete idiots dressed like sales reps and driving brand new Mondeos to Moscow should consider staying there.

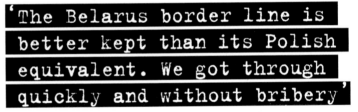

'The Belarus border line is better kept than its Polish equivalent. We got through quickly and without bribery'

Next morning, it took no time to get to the Belarus border and then I started to feel some nerves. Not because we were entering Europe's last dictatorship – an official member of Condoleezza Rice's 'Outposts of Tyranny', thanks to president Alex Lukashenko's antics – but because not crossing this frontier would mean the end of the story.

A mile-long line of Belarus-plated vehicles sat stationary, waiting to cross the border – many of these were old and dusty VW Transporters with curtained windows and generally more than three people in the back when you could see in. The rest were old Audi 100s. If you've ever wondered

it was time to cross the murky waters of the Bug. Heading away from the Polish line and toward the Belarus line, we were officially in no-man's-land, a bit of territory that belongs to neither country. Spooky.

The Belarus border line is better kept than its Polish equivalent. Our paperwork was in order, no bribery was required and we were into Belarus in less than half the time it took us to leave Poland.

Past Brest with its gleaming white tower blocks and into the undulating open steppe, the Mondeo cruised easily in strange surroundings. Well, here we go. Europe's last dictatorship. I thought about nuclear weapon silos,

UWAGA !
KOLCZATKA

PROSIMY CZEKAĆ
NA
WYDANIE PRZEPUSTKI

Nerves at one of the
border crossings. Time to
take out some US dollars?

Firing up the Mondeo, as it bombs through the surprisingly friendly Belarus

atomic research facilities, toxic waste and people with three heads, none of which were in evidence.

I wasn't going to break the 75 mph limit. 'We don't know the situation in Belarus and neither do you' was a constant mantra in my head, and speeding in a full-on dictatorship took on a new resonance, somehow. The motorway opened out into a smooth four-lane highway, newly-built and mostly empty apart from long convoys of mostly Russian trucks escorted by small police cars. This is a fast and excellent road.

However, leaving the M1 in Belarus is the most amazing thing about it. After 10 yards, the tarmac disappears and you're onto dirt tracks through farming villages, where chickens battled with the Mondeo for road space. Photographer Alex Puczniec took a photo of a nice old couple sitting on a bench, and it immediately started a blazing argument with a neighbour. She yelled at the top of her voice that they shouldn't allow their photo to be taken because they had no idea where it would be used.

'Ah, ignore her,' said the old peasant to Alex in perfect Polish. 'All she does is yell at us all day. Hey,' he shouted at his neighbour, 'why don't you take your knickers off? That'll make him take your picture!'

The people we encountered in these villages, from schoolkids to farmers to girls wearing white high-heel cowboy boots, were all friendly and happy and wonderful, amused by my bad sunglasses ('1981, Audi Quattro launch,' I'd say to them) and completely oblivious of the car.

Minsk, the Belarus capital and our overnight stop, with its open squares and old buildings, reminded me of Paris a little bit – except much cleaner and better organised. No shortage of money, either, as

All along the road to
Moscow are war memorials,
evidence of the struggles
against the Nazis in WW2

The M1 as you are never
likely to see it in
England. Pure bliss

evidenced by streets packed with modern western cars. Seems like Belarus consists of two countries in one – Minsk and the rest of it. The architecture is interesting once you leave the massed apartment blocks of the suburbs and reach the old town, and things are geared up well for tourists, with plenty of museums and music and art and culture to check out. The streets seem safe, quiet and unthreatening. We didn't see any dictators.

Next morning, we took a risk and upped the speed. The Mondeo is unflustered by bumps and big undulations at high speed, even on its softest suspension setting. The last model was great but this one is better in every way possible.

We turned off the M1 again seeking adventure and ended up in a farming area behind a large house – the owner, a 70-year-old with kind black eyes and a handshake like an iron vice, explained that the large rocket in his back yard was a bomb casing, a relic from the Second World War. Where between London and Leeds could you meet a bloke with a big bomb in his back yard?

Passing from Belarus to Russia was far more difficult than the crossing from Poland into Belarus. Form after form was filled in and copied and presented to various people in the border 'complex', which again consisted of Portakabins. Even with the help of an angry Russian on the other end of a mobile phone, it took two hours and $500 to get over. If the border crossing from Lithuania isn't easier, I can't see how anyone would consider driving into Russia.

Kolya met us in a Bentley Flying Spur, parked in the far corner of a run-down shack of a petrol station. Kolya doesn't do things by halves. He and his second-in-command, Nikolay, produced a giant tapped container of vodka and dropped it onto the Bentley's bonnet. This is more like a welcome. Suddenly the horrific over-officious border crossing was a distant memory.

'Welcome to Russia,' said Kolya, lining up the shot glasses. 'So, who is driving?'

I replied that I was, so I didn't get a shot. There is no leeway with drink driving in Russia: if the police detect even a trace of alcohol on you, your license is confiscated along with your car and you go to the nearest lock-up.

'Ah, and look here,' said Kolya, walking round to the rear of the car. The boot lid eased up on its electric motor and inside were some machine pistols and various handguns. 'You see, I told you we had our own guns! We go!'

The motorway 'services' on this stretch of the M1 seem to sell, almost exclusively, fish. One services we stopped at had a line of 20 stalls and all sold smoked fish. I'll never criticise Watford Gap services again.

There are war memorials all the way to Moscow, of course – some with sculptures and statues, others with tanks and guns. Remember the Soviet Union lost 27 million souls in the Second World War, compared with 'only' 650,000 British and American war dead combined. That's 41 times the casualties. It makes you hope for a bright future for this country.

From Smolensk, we speared toward Moscow in the grey driving rain, the Mondeo and Spur rolling in easy convoy along a single-lane road that passed through a gigantic fir tree forest for hour after hour. Sorry, but there's nothing to say about this stretch of the M1, mainly because there's nothing there. The stand-out highlight was a fake wooden police car at the road edge.

A thick mass of apartment blocks welcomed us to the outskirts of Moscow, then we drove through a central district as fascinating as any

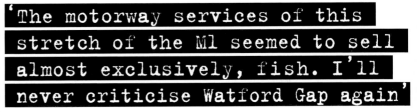

'The motorway services of this stretch of the M1 seemed to sell almost exclusively, fish. I'll never criticise Watford Gap again'

city on earth. The Moscovites I met were all great people – blessed with an almost Latin expressiveness and a true passion for life.

The M1 ended not too far from Red Square, so we parked the Mondeo there for a final photo. As I looked at the Ford sitting proudly in front of St Basil's Cathedral, I couldn't help thinking that this superb car was the true star of the trip. It protected us so effectively from the children with Kalashnikovs and the violent police and the corrupt soldiers and the bandits and the firing squads and radiation and nukes, it was almost as if these nasty threats didn't exist in the first place. Leeds to London? Pah! No problem. Bring it on.

MERCEDES POSSESSED

Vehicle: Mercedes-Benz CL63 AMG
Climate: Dark, oh so very dark
Distance: 1,046 miles
Duration: 4 days and dark nights
Road Surface: Tarmac under mist
Roadkill Roulette: 6 bats, 13 rats, an entire pack of wolves
Notes:
The Mercedes CL63 AMG is a car that practises the dark arts of engineering. Only one place to take it then – the home of Dracula.

Chapter 10

Velcome to Transylvania

The stealth-like Merc CL63 is the only car that can match Transylvania for brooding presence. Bring the two of them together and who knows what may be unleashed

Words Matt Master Photography by Lee Brimble

SALIVA WHIPPING ABOUT ITS JOWLS, A SCRAWNY BLACK DOG is chasing down the car. Bolting from doorways and ditches, others join him, teeth bared, matted fur bristling.

Crawling through Arefu, villagers scurry for the sanctuary of dark rooms, doors slam shut and curtains are drawn. A small child is snatched up by its father and bundled into the back of a cart. As I pull alongside, our eyes meet for a moment and then he turns, blank and ashen.

Bowing the casement of a third floor window, a group of teenage schoolgirls jostle for the ideal position, whistling and giggling over the sound of the engine. Looking up, I catch the glance of a slight, dark-haired creature, china-white skin against dark-red lips. Her wink is the Devil's work, a Faustian pact, penetrating deep into the car's cabin. A bell clangs beyond and suddenly she's vanished, replaced by a burly matron who crashes the windowpanes together with short, thick forearms and yanks a blind down between us...

The evening before, high on the hill behind Arefu, the winter sun shines weakly, its last rays shooting between the branches of birches and the battlements of Cetatea Poienari. After three days and 1,500 miles, I have arrived.

This is the Arges region of Transylvania, a place unmolested by the 21st century. Or the 20th come to that. Here, old women till the soil into their nineties and the wealthier households have a horse and cart. Smoke still rises from every chimney and pork, potatoes and cabbage remain the dietary staple.

Poienari Citadel was built in 1459, when Vlad Tepes marched a captured community of Turks up the Arges Valley and worked every single one of them to death on its construction. With its bloody legacy behind him, it was from here that Vlad waged war on the invading Turks for a decade, earning his legendary monicker 'The Impaler'. Although fond of boiling his enemies, or burying them alive, his real signature was to insert a wooden stake into his victim's anus, driving it out just below the shoulder in such a way as to avoid damaging any major organs.

His father, Vlad II, was awarded the chivalric Order of the Dragon in the year of his son's birth. From then on known as Vlad Dracul, meaning dragon, he gave his heir the affectionate nickname 'Son of the dragon', or Draculea.

Making the final ascent to his castle, it becomes clear I am a little late. In 1462, the Turks laid a final siege to Poienari. Dracula's wife flung herself

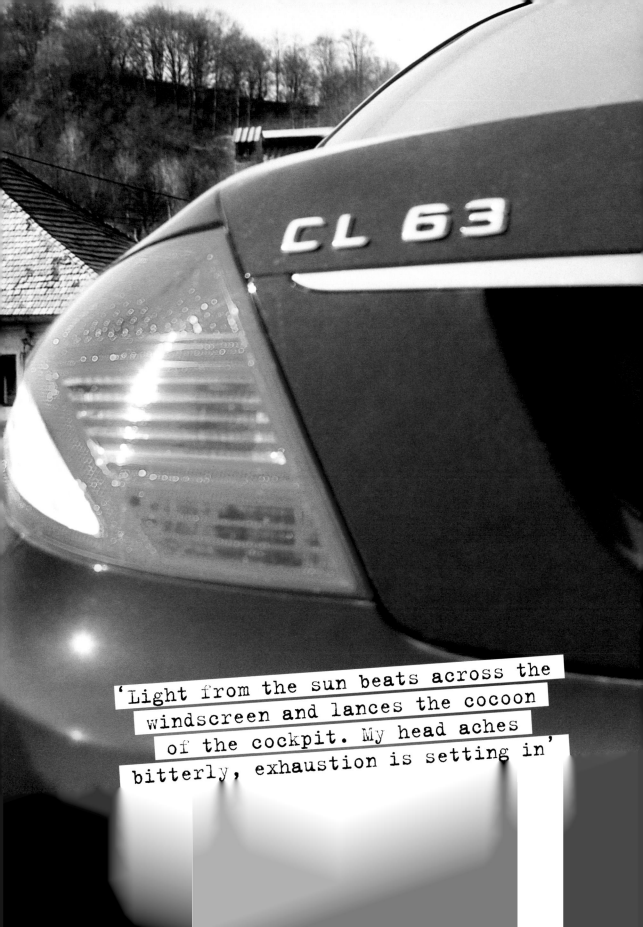

'Light from the sun beats across the windscreen and lances the cocoon of the cockpit. My head aches bitterly, exhaustion is setting in'

seeping into every leaden limb as I point the vast black bonnet of the Mercedes north for the Hungarian border and home.

An hour short of Arad, the road is blocked. Police cars and decrepit Eastern Bloc ambulances weave their way through lines of traffic to a macabre scene playing itself out beyond sight a mile up the road. They return as the sun begins to set behind me, their red lights pulsing in the gloom and an alien wail of unfamiliar sirens drifting off towards Sibiu with their terrible cargo.

After a total of two hours stationary, the lorry in front begins to roll forwards and we all slowly snake up the mountain, past a single officer of the local Politia, a yellow Trabant facing the wrong way and a figure lying motionless in the verge. His blue chequered shirt is pulled up over his face, concealing his final expression from the living and revealing an expanse of bloated, hairless flesh. In the ditch beside him is an angry twist of indeterminate wreckage, a vague automotive epitaph.

I wind the CL in a crawling convoy over a final alpine crest, the Transylvanian sun disappearing for the last time behind the summit. Zig-zagging down, the road begins to open up for overtaking.

At the border a uniformed guard stares long and hard at my passport in the twilight. He runs a torch the length of the CL's brutal, black profile before pointing it straight into my bloodshot eyes. With a step back he murmurs

> **'People have been reacting differently all day. Is it me or is it the car? At this point, to be honest, we are one and the same'**

something and waves me quickly through. People have been reacting differently all day. Seeing something strange and dangerous, something other worldly. Is it me or is it the car? At this point, to be honest, we are one and the same. A shared purpose, a mutual dependence. A pact with our own devil.

Nightfall is complete on entering Hungary and the tiredness abates. I'm gripped instead with a sense of urgency; finding dual carriageway for the first time in hours, then motorway for the first time in days. My focus is simply for miles, and the car finally touches its limiter as it spears the empty autostrada towards Budapest. I'm a new man now, night shrouding car and driver, the rapid drop in temperature assisting our collective progress. The occasional artic appears as two red eyes on the horizon before rapidly vanishing behind us with an audible thump of displaced air. This is our natural environment, the moment when we understand each other, work together, are utterly untouchable. Sleep could not be less important, any hesitation in our progress an abhorrent impossibility. Unhindered by the clutter of day, CL63 and driver find common ground. A car like this cannot live alongside others, destined instead to cross continents under the cover of night. I am bringing something haunting but beautiful home with me. Something most people will not understand. Something most people will seek to avoid. This prince of darkness.

The Mercedes waits for nightfall and a chance to enjoy itself

Vehicle: Jaguar XKR
Climate: A bit fraught
Distance: 2,768 miles
Duration: 3 long days and nights
Road Surface: Interstate concrete
Roadkill Roulette: All manner of
night critters. But no cops
Notes:
America is a country built around
the mythology of the open road. So
where better to let your hair down
in a rather flash Jaguar XKR?

Chapter 11.

Jaguar takes on Middle America

The Jaguar XKR has an arresting quality – it's the speed of the thing. But driving across the flat, featureless midwest, what's there to do but put your foot down?

Words Pat Devereux Photography by Alex P and Lee Brimble

THERE'S A TINY BLUE CRYSTAL SPARKLING IN MY rearview mirror. I think it's the projector headlights of Tom Ford in the S-Type behind me, as it's been there a while now and it's not been getting any bigger. It may even be shrinking. That's OK, he'll catch up at the next fuel stop. I squeeze the throttle of the XKR a little harder, then a little harder still, until the pedal is all the way to the floor. The engine bellows with delight – it's a much deeper note than that of the non-supercharged engines – and we spear forward through the pitch-black Texas night as fast as this new Jaguar will go. Nice. We'll soon have that average speed reading back where it should be.

Driving at night makes a lot of sense when you are in the middle part of the US. There's very little to see in the day other than endless, flat plains stretching off in every direction. It's quite bizarre driving across them in daylight as the outside scenery doesn't seem to change – or the

> **'We spear forward through the pitch-black night as fast as this new Jaguar will go. Nice. We'll soon have that average speed back where it should be'**

horizon get any closer – however fast you go. It looks exactly the same at 175mph as it does at 65, only the verge is a little more blurry. Just how the settlers managed to make it all the way to the west coast on a horse and cart without dying from boredom or inbreeding is a true mystery. They don't call these 'flyover' states for nothing.

Ask any mathematician what the keys to a good average time are and – if you can stay awake – they'll tell you it's not just about stopping as few times as possible. It's also about being able to regain your cruising speed in minimum time. And that's something the XKR, which we're discovering is a quite brilliant GT car, is deeply able to do. Subtract a few mph coming into a corner or to avoid a car in front and it's no problem as you can add them again and resume your cruise the moment the road is open once more.

It's rare to find such power in a device as comfortable as this Jag, so we are now making full use of both. Well, I am. Alex, the photographer, has fallen fast asleep. Great. Here we are belting across a barren wasteland in the dead of night with no chance of sleep for me for at least six more hours and my wingman is hibernating next to me. Well, he does wake occasionally, but only to spout a stream of extreme gibberish, shift into a more comfortable position and, sometimes, fart loudly before drifting off again.

So I have to amuse myself, which, to be honest, isn't terribly hard to do in this car. First question to answer – is the top speed limited, like the

The perfect food to keep you going on the highway

GREAT FOR LOW CARB DIETS

BEEF JERKY

makers claim? Hang on a minute... er, no, it's clearly not. Not unless the speedo is seriously over-reading and, even if it is, I'm still impressed as the needle has almost run out of numbers to point at. Alex, none the wiser of this huge velocity, sighs deeply and turns onto his side. Next question, and probably more important as a truck is breaking ranks and pulling out up ahead, is the R's braking performance from high speed. I stand lightly on the brake pedal and the force is sufficient to draw us up well before the truck – and make Alex slump lifelessly into the footwell, like a fried egg out of a pan, without waking up. They work nicely, too, then.

Unlike the radar detector, which is squarking madly at nothing, and the headlights on Tom's S-Type R chase car – which is slowing down because that truck has allowed him to make up a bit of ground, so now I can see the lamps a bit more clearly and they really don't seem to be

> **'I'm declared the fastest nick they've ever had. The cop then shakes my hand and thanks me for being so courteous. Too weird'**

working properly. They look... OH. MY. GOD. It's not Wookie! Those aren't projector headlights, they are the blue flashing lights of a cop car. Hang on, there's more than one. Oh no. There's another right behind it and – oh, God – another behind that, too. That, as any decent mathematician will tell you, makes three.

This is going to be bad. Prison bad.

With a knot the size of a football forming in my stomach, I pull the Jaguar over to the hard shoulder and wait for the inevitable knock on the window. When it comes, it isn't the angry belt from a nightstick. It's a soft tap from a gloved hand attached to a Texas cop, smiling disbelievingly.

'You know what the speed limit on this road is, sir?' he says. I deadpan it and tell him I do, plus, to help defuse things a bit, that I may have been going a little faster than that.

'A little faster?' he says. 'Sir, my car is limited to 131mph. I've been following you for 12 miles and you were pulling away from me fast. If that truck hadn't pulled out back there I reckon you'd have crossed the state line before we could have caught up with you. Then you'd have been free.'

I don't like the sound of the 'then you'd have been free' bit. Implies I'm not going to be for much longer. Which proves to be the case.

'I'm going to have to take you down to the court house and charge you,' he says.

Not quite sure what to say, or what's going to happen, I settle for a nod

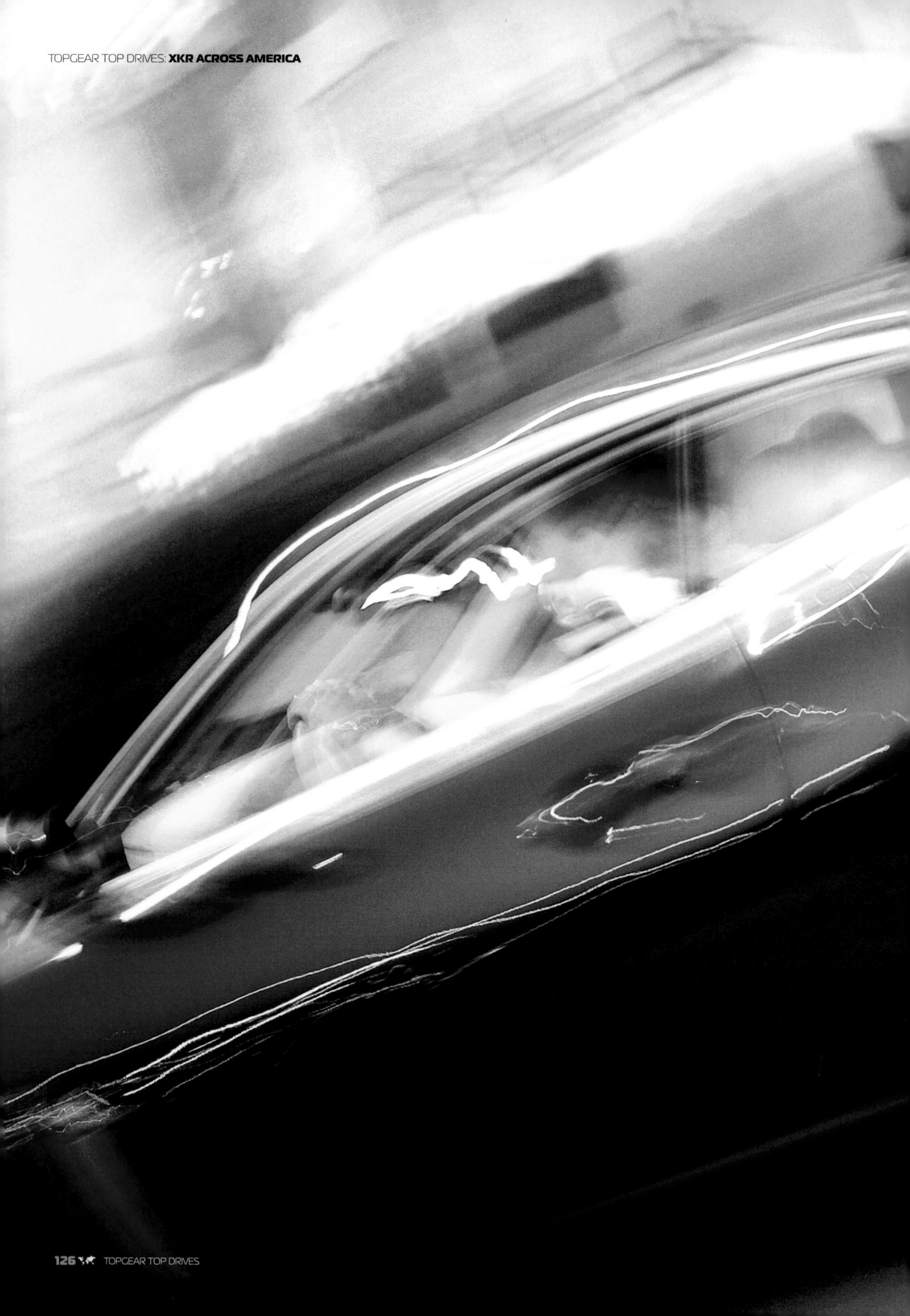

of acknowledgement. Following his over-worked, under-powered cruiser in the relaxed, suitably powered new XKR through a deep ditch at the side of the road and back to the court house, I have to force myself not to think about all the cop movies I've seen over the years. 'Ha, you goin' to get it hard with a nightstick, bo-ah!' says Alex.

'Is this him?' says the woman behind the glass partition when I walk into the court house, which turns out to be the cop shop, too.

'Yeah, this is him,' says the cop. 'Got him at 125mph.' Great. I'm notorious already. But I'm hopeful because the speed is a lot lower than it might have been. 'Is he a 296?' she says. 'Yeah, a 296,' he says tiredly. I ask what a '296' is, thinking it's a code for 'death by hanging' or 'firing squad', and I'm told very matter-of-factly that it's the amount of the fine I'm going to have to pay. Positive thoughts race through my mind: what, just a fine? And only 300 bucks? Value! They aren't going to impound

That needle is climbing a tad too high... Oops, too late

> **'By comparison, the rest of the journey is uneventful. Except I get a ticket from a cop for not indicating at a bend in the road!'**

the car – or put me away? I screw up my face to hide the smile that's trying to rip my visage in half. 'Whew,' I say. 'That's a lot of money!'

Unbelievably, things get better and better from there on, to the point that, once all the paperwork is finished – and I'm declared the fastest nick they've ever had – the cop has a sit in the new Jag and gazes over the leather. 'We could do with a couple of these,' he says looking lustfully at the dash. 'Could catch pretty much anyone in one of these.' He's not wrong – he could. But not now as we have a clock to chase and need our car back asap, please. So he shakes my hand, thanks me for 'being so courteous' and waves us on our way. Even offers to buy us a cup of coffee if we stop by next time we are passing. It's all too weird for words. Even Alex's words.

By comparison, the rest of the journey to Flagstaff is positively, and thankfully, uneventful. The last bit of Texas passes without further ado. We – sorry, I – get a 'courtesy ticket' from a traffic cop in New Mexico for not indicating for a bend in the road – I'm serious.

We pull into Flagstaff feeling surprisingly OK. Despite all the police attention and buggering about with paperwork, thanks to the XKR's frankly amazing ability to vault us across huge tracts of the country in supreme comfort, we are not that far behind schedule. We can still make it if we're quick. Just need to watch out for those blue crystals and we should be fine.

No sign of flashing blue
lights in this wing mirror.
Just a criminally good sunset
on the American west coast

higher than that of the UK – but prohibitive car tax excludes the exotic. No one can ever remember a Lamborghini visiting these shores before, which is why our arrival has been akin to that of Dr Livingstone – '*Top Gear*, I presume.' The TV show is hugely popular here and our visit made headline news in one of the local newspapers. Their only disappointment is that I'm not Clarkson (who has a Gallardo of his own), Hammond or May.

Situated halfway between Scotland and Iceland in the middle of the North Atlantic, the Faroe Islands are an extraordinary place. They're home to just 48,000 people but they boast their own language and their own bank notes. Officially, the Islands are part of the Kingdom of Denmark, but their parliament has autonomy over local issues.

For a place of such natural beauty, the Faroes receive little attention. Part of the problem is their remote location. We left London on Friday, drove to Perth and then on to Aberdeen, where we caught an overnight ferry to the Shetlands.

'As a long-distance tool, the Lambo is surprisingly capable. Gone are the days when it was considered pretty but useless'

'Is that Lamborghini real?' asked a ferryman. 'We thought it might have been one of them replicas.'

After eight hours in the Shetlands we caught a second and surprisingly plush ferry to the Faroes. Next year, the local Smyril Line will open a direct ferry route from Scotland, which will make life easier. There are plenty of flights, but a Gallardo might fall foul of hand baggage restrictions.

As a long-distance tool, the Lambo is surprisingly capable. Gone are the days when it was the automotive equivalent of a poster-boy dunderhead – pretty but useless. The purists might bemoan the company's German ownership but there can be no denying that it has resulted in a much better Lamborghini.

After the Shetlands – a place so grey it looks like it's been desaturated – the Faroes adds a welcome dash of colour. Quaint wooden buildings are dotted around Torshavn's pretty harbour and many boast roofs made of turf. 'When we want to cut the grass, we just throw up a couple of sheep,' says a local, half-joking. The vibe is laid-back and surprisingly cool – very Scandinavian.

The local jet-wash is run by Jakup Borg, who plays in midfield for the Faroes football team. 'I had a month-long trial with Liverpool in 1998,' he says. 'I've also played for the Faroes against Germany but Michael Ballack wouldn't swap shirts, his attitude was, "Who are you?"'

Like many of the Faroese we've met, Borg seems content. 'There's no crime,' he says. 'Tórshavn is a good place to be – there are eight bars and four nightclubs – but some of the other communities feel like they're stuck in the Sixties or Seventies. There's not much going on with them.'

Sleepy fishing villages
are what the Faroes are
all about. But the Lambo
is about to change all that

'The landscape is aggressive. Its jagged coastlines

look as if some mythical giant had nibbled at them'

Our Lamborghini has been disparagingly described as a 'footballer's car', but this is to do it a disservice. Sitting soaking on the garage floor, it rekindles memories of the original Countach, before it was polluted by wings and scoops. It's a refreshingly pure design that works well from every angle, hood up or down.

But such beauty is not achieved without compromise and Borg laughs out loud when I open the boot. The cubby in the nose is so small that my luggage for a week's trip has been reduced to two tatty carrier bags. From day three onwards, I'll be forced to wear my underpants inside out.

After posing for an inevitable picture, we leave the affable Borg to his labour and head for the hills. The scenery in the Faroe Islands is different to that of northern Scotland or the Shetland Islands. It's much more aggressive, with steep gradients and jagged coastlines, as if some other-worldly being has nibbled at giant chunks of earth and left the rest to rot.

> 'In the early '90s, the Faroes government built tunnels that link most of the 18 islands. It's beautiful, supercar nirvana'

In the early '90s the Faroes' government built tunnels that link most of the 18 islands. Much of the traffic now takes the underground route, which has left some of the more dramatic roads deserted. The one that runs northwest from Tórshavn is seminal. Stretching for some 12miles, it criss-crosses the hillside before plunging down the valley. Wide and beautifully surfaced, it's supercar nirvana.

With the roof down, the sonorous cry of the 520bhp engine is much more accessible. I slot-shift to second and put my foot down. The Gallardo scoops itself up and flings itself at the horizon. The pub-bore stats – 0–60mph takes just 4.3 secs and a top whack of 195mph – tell only part of the tale. The throttle response is angry and immediate and the manual 'box hops from cog-to-cog with a metallic ping that's hugely emotive.

At high speed, the Alcantara steering wheel chats like an adolescent on a first date, while the suspension flatters the bumpy surface. My fears that the chop-top Gallardo would be no more than a boulevard playboy are dispatched in an instant. So much of the coupé's grace and favour has been retained, but now it's been given a more earthy quality. You interact with this car like no Lamborghini before it.

This road leads to the tiny communities that line the northern coastline and on day two we pay them an impromptu visit. Tiny gaggles of grass-roofed houses, often no more than 20, cling to the seashore. Most of these hamlets possess a church but nothing else. 'We have to travel half an hour for milk,' explains a resident of Gjógv. Parked beside these houses,

the Lamborghini has never looked more incongruous and its soundtrack makes me feel self-conscious.

Given the paucity of entertainment and the relative affluence of the population, it's no surprise to discover a buoyant car culture. 'A car in the Faroe Islands is either transport from A to B or a flat in which you socialise,' Djurholm tells me. 'In small communities, there is nowhere to meet.' At night, local youths lap the streets of Tórshavn in a steady procession.

The cruisers are magnetically drawn to the Lamborghini. Word has spread of where we're staying and each night our hotel is besieged by groups of young people, desperate to pose by our toy. Even the local police turn up for a gawp and they're joined by a group of bikers. 'In the Faroes motorbike tax is not so high and even a 20-year-old can have a superbike,' says Jakup Djurhuvs. 'One of our friends was killed last week, but we do not learn.' I'm challenged to a race but think better of it.

For some locals, this passion for all things automotive has become an obsession. On day three, we're introduced to Sofus Hansen, nicknamed Fuzzy. The

> 'Word has spread about the Lambo; each night our hotel is under seige from young locals eager to pose for a photo by our toy'

Faroes' only car-builder operates out of a tiny garage beneath his house. Fuzzy earns a decent living spray painting cars, but bespoke coachwork is his primary art. A restyled Harley sits beside a Porsche 928 that's been crossed with a Peugeot 407. The results may not be to all tastes, but there's no doubting the craftsmanship. 'People think I'm a crazy playboy,' he says.

Fuzzy also has a niece. Ever since we arrived, we've been noticing the strength of the Faroese gene pool and Barbara Carlsen is its crowning glory. She works in the mayor's office in Tórshavn but has achieved local fame by singing in a gospel choir. 'The Faroes is boring,' she complains as she inspects the Gallardo, 'there's nothing here to do.' I nod pathetically. Faced with exceptional beauty, I've forgotten how to speak.

Our meeting proves a fitting climax to what has been a fascinating few days. Like Barbara, the Faroes are small but beautifully formed.

We left London a week ago not sure what we'd find. There was a danger that we'd be bored by the Faroes and irritated by the Gallardo's impracticality, but both have exceeded our expectations. The Faroe Islands probably aren't the most exciting place in which to grow up, but they're a great place to visit and the roads are terrific.

The baby Lamborghini has also sustained my interest. The Gallardo is a brilliantly engineered tool that doesn't rely on its supermodel looks to seduce. Home is seven hundred miles away, and I'm looking forward to every one.

'We left London not sure what we'd find. But the Faroes are a great place to visit. And it has terrific roads'

IND

THE BEETLE IN INDIA

Vehicle: 1970 Volkswagen Beetle
Climate: Hazy
Distance: 634 miles
Duration: 4 days and nights
Road Surface: Well spaced
Roadkill Roulette: Not a thing.
All life is sacred around here
Notes:
The Beatles came to Rishikesh in
northern India back in 1968. We join
the magical mystery tour in pursuit
and get far out in a VW Beetle.

Chapter 13

Beetlemania in northern India

In 1968, the Beatles came to the yoga capital of India to meditate on the meaning of life. Another Sixties icon, the VW Beetle is our transport as we make our pilgrimage

Words Rob Bright Photography by Barry Hayden

TWO HOURS BACK, A COUPLE OF JEWEL-EYED TRIPPERS drank coffee laced with pharmaceutical-grade LSD and the first thing they start to notice are the details; how the folds in their jeans are charged with symbolism both profound and ineffable; how an unseen cosmic prompt has caused the grain in the wood of the table to flow like a river; how the walls of the room are vibrating. What else? Oh yeah, purple flares and paisley shirts – they can't quite work out the reason why but a man simply had to have them.

The year is 1965 and the two trippers in question are John Lennon and George Harrison. They've just joined the growing band of merry pranksters in the West who have been turned on to acid, the psychedelic drug reputed to unlock the door to ancient mysteries and to provide a wake-up call from God. From this point onwards in their artistic careers, The Beatles' music will never be the same again.

So, where are we now? The future. 2007. A time of teleportation pods and cloud cities. Well, not quite, but times have changed. I'm driving down an Indian road full of colour and dust, dodging ox carts and rickshaws, over-taking buses that might fall to bits if you look at them for too long, yet manage to transport, seemingly, the equivalent of the population of Albania. And all the time I'm leaning on the horn, begging any and all of the country's few thousand gods to keep me from crashing, feeling part of some automotive ballet where I missed the rehearsals.

We are heading to Rishikesh in northern India, yoga capital of the world, in a 1971 VW Beetle with chrome livery and painted flames on the bonnet. The car is the blatant hook of the story; to take the Love Bug to one of the Love Generation's old haunts, a Beetle to the place made famous by The Beatles. It's really that simple.

When The Beatles came here in 1968, joining the Maharishi at his ashram on the banks of the Ganges, they were continuing a trend that began in the late Fifties. They had just released the Sgt Pepper album, the one that defined psychedelia, and were hailed by the high priest of LSD, Timothy Leary, as messengers from God. More and more people had been turning on to acid, crowding into camper vans with Day-Glo paint jobs, heading for Haight-Ashbury, La Honda, Millbrook, Glastonbury... But for others it wasn't enough. The further they looked into themselves, the further from home they seemed to get. Some of them got as far as Kathmandu, travelling from Europe through Turkey, Iran, Afghanistan, Pakistan and India, before arriving burnt-out or transformed in Nepal. It became the original hippy trail, and Rishikesh was one of its principal ports of call.

But that was then. Anyone after the same trip in 2007 ought to steel themselves for some bad vibes once they wave goodbye to Turkey, maybe strap on a flak-jacket under the kaftan past Iran. As The Beatles put it on *The White Album,* written mainly in India, 'happiness is a warm gun'.

There are some parts of the 155mile journey from Delhi to Rishikesh where a gun on the dashboard might be just the ticket, so an Indian friend tells me – car-jacking is commonplace. At the moment, though, the busy two-lane highway poses other problems, as one of India's most terrifying vehicles hurtles towards us: the public carrier. Camouflaged in a riot of Indian gods, floral patterns and tinsel, and crammed with wild-eyed men in torn undershirts and grubby bandanas – with yet more bidi-smoking lunatics clinging to its roof – it approaches head-on, lights flashing, using a horn with the depth and grandeur of a transatlantic cruise ship.

Another resident of Rishikesh fond of living the high life

'The truck passes by, inches away, the Doppler effect from its horn providing a fitting analogue for the feeling in my gut'

My foot is already buried to the floor as I urge the car past the coach we are trying to overtake. It's going to be close. Time stretches out, offers up its cinematic slow-mo' finale, and just when I'm sure it's too late, that this time it's oblivion, I manage to swerve back into the left-hand lane. The truck passes by in a blur of colour, inches away, the Doppler effect from the horn providing a fitting analogue for the feeling in my gut.

It's just another close shave. One of hundreds, even thousands that happen every day. On this road, as on any in India, you get the impression that the entire history of transport is being played out in a single, chaotic moment; bullock carts, horse-drawn carriages, bicycles, pedal and auto-rickshaws, tractors, motorbikes, cars, trucks, buses – all manner of vehicles are competing for space, the rules that govern them lost in the fog of exhaust fumes and the fury of engines. And given the huge variations in speed, overtaking is constant. After six hours it's finally over and we are in Rishikesh. I feel like I need a few shots of 'Knock-Out whisky' from a local liquor store or a spliff the size of an ice-cream cone. The meditation can wait until tomorrow.

For The Beatles it was the other way around. Rishikesh was a much needed escape from the drug-fuelled chaos that had erupted around them, as well as a means of coping with manager Brian Epstein's death and the cracks that were beginning to show in the group. John Lennon needed a break from LSD. He had spent the last two years glugging back all the God-given truth oil he could lay his hands on. While tripping in his den he would put on headphones and listen to recitations of the Tibetan Book of

Everyone gets a buzz out of seeing the Beetle, a true retro classic

'The Beetle fitted right in with the whole counter-culture, what with its art nouveau curves and kitschy bazaar-art styling'

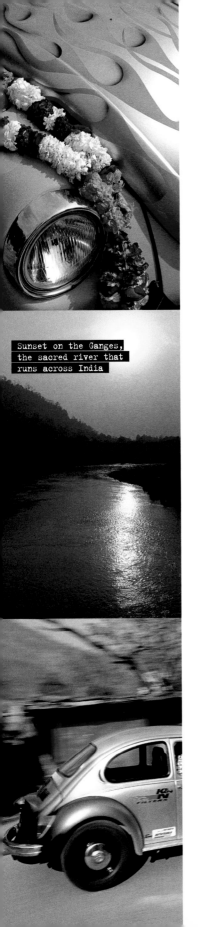

Sunset on the Ganges, the sacred river that runs across India

the Dead. At Abbey Road, he was asking producer George Martin to make sounds 'orange' and at one point he thought he was a reincarnation of Jesus and wanted an official statement put out to that effect. McCartney, ever the team player, saw the Rishikesh trip as something they could do together, a sort of bonding exercise. He had tried acid, but preferred the subtler effects of cannabis. Harrison was the most sincere, having picked up an interest in ancient Indian Vedic philosophy and yoga a few years earlier. He'd turned his back on LSD after going to Haight-Ashbury in San Francisco, and being mobbed by all the long-haired, sunken-faced freaks filling up the sidewalks, claiming him as their messiah. Ringo, being Ringo, just commented dryly that the whole ashram thing felt a bit like Butlins.

The town's name 'Rishikesh' translates as 'Hair of Sages', with obvious appeal to the Westerners arriving in the Sixties and Seventies. As the hazy sun rises over the river, we drive the Beetle down from the hill spa where we have been staying, our progress watched by monkeys scavenging at the roadside. The car's owner, Raj Kapoor, has warned us about a few of its inevitable idiosyncrasies. He just uses it for cruising about town, he tells us, and is worried about what might happen to it on such a long drive. He's sent his mechanic along to keep an eye on it – or maybe an eye on me, worried that I might attempt handbrake turns on hairpins down the mountain or some such extravagance. As it is, we take it easy, but there are strange sounds emitting from somewhere near the left front wheel when I put on the brakes or we go over bumps.

> **'As the sun rises over the river, we drive the Beetle down from the hill spa, watched by monkeys scavenging at the roadside'**

Still, the engine is bubbling away sweetly and there's no rush. We make it down the mountain and into Rishikesh, arousing amusement and wonder among the locals. A gang of schoolkids want their photograph taken with it, saffron-robed *sadhus* (holy men) are jolted from trances to cast a glance in our direction and backpacking Westerners give approving smiles and thumbs-ups. The kitschy bazaar-art style of the paintwork sees it fit right in here, just as the Beetle did with the whole counterculture aesthetic of the Sixties, what with its quasi-art nouveau curves and an overall shape that echoes a pod or an egg – forms that set the primal neurons firing in the stoned brain. Back then, its reputation was also enhanced by the fact that it could reputedly perform miracles like float on water – at least for a little while – thanks to its tight door seals, while in the same year the Fab Four arrived in Rishikesh, Herbie was putting in his very first appearance for Disney in *The Love Bug*. It's one of those curious ironies, then, that the car's production was only made possible by financial backing from the Nazi Party in the Thirties.

But then, history isn't short on irony. *The White Album* was largely the product of the two months The Beatles spent at the Maharishi's ashram, meditating on time and timelessness, the I and the not-I, using yoga to dissolve dualities into a great ocean of harmony and oneness. And yet it's the same album that Charles Manson interpreted as a personal message sent to him about the coming apocalypse, and that resulted in his disciples committing murder on Hollywood's boulevards, lyrics from the album written in victims' blood on the walls of their houses.

In truth, the period The Beatles spent in Rishikesh was a profound turning point; the Summer of Love of 1967 was over, the Tet Offensive in Vietnam underway. In April, The Beatles returned disillusioned from India after allegations that the Maharishi had made sexual advances towards one of the female entourage (which inspired the song 'Sexy Sadie'). In the same month, Martin Luther King was assassinated, then Bobby Kennedy a couple of months later; while on the streets of Paris students were fighting running battles with the police. As for the hippies, the bad trips were multiplying, and the entire movement was already being rapidly assimilated and trivialised by the juggernaut that was the consumer boom. As Danny from *Withnail and I* put it, 'They're selling hippy wigs in Woolworths, man...'

And so time rolls on, as do I, driving at walking pace down bustling streets, India in all its contradictions streaming across the windscreen; bronze gods and internet cafes, luminous saris and snow-wash jeans; faces hidden behind

'The period The Beatles spent at Rishikesh was a profound turning point; the Summer of Love was over, the Tet Offensive under way'

veils or D&G sunglasses. Eventually, we emerge into Triveni Ghat: an area with steps leading to the river where Hindus gather to worship every evening or disperse the ashes of their loved ones, and in so doing release them from the cycle of rebirth. Light explodes off the silver roof and bonnet of the Beetle. People start to gather round, including a couple of *sadhus* who have no issue with us taking their photographs in the car, provided we pay them well enough. After some aggressive bartering we reach a fair price.

I get back in the driver's seat, push the car into the first of its four gears, grab the large thin steering wheel and set off in the direction of one of the two bridges that cross the Ganges, where we take some more shots watched by bleary-eyed stoneheads. We park up to grab some lunch, but when we try to get the car started again, it refuses. The engine has overheated and Raj's mechanic looks concerned. Given that Raj went to great lengths to give us the car in the first place, we decide to accept it as fate and the car is loaded onto a support truck, a typically Indian act of improvisation involving sandbags, some lengths of 4x2, GCSE carpentry skills and lots of good karma.

As a sun like an orange pill falls behind the trees and dissolves into a pink sky, I reflect on the fact that 40 years on, Westerners are still coming to places like this, many of them to get high, a few looking for answers. What The Beatles found here was expressed in iconic songs like 'Revolution', 'Dear Prudence' and 'Julia', among others. And, like the band, the Beetle is forever bound to that decade when everything was in flux, and the only way to approach it was to 'turn off your mind, relax and float downstream'.

The great Indian art of improvisation sure beats the AA

Safely stowed on the truck,
the Beetle reflects on its
time chanting mantras on
the banks of the Ganges

हापुड़
HAPUR 37

बुलन्दशहर
BULANDSHAHR 52

NH 24

< NBA >

CRUISING THE DUNES

Vehicle: Toyota Land Cruiser
Climate: Sandy and sizzling
Distance: 567 miles
Duration: 4 days and starry nights
Road Surface: Grainy
Roadkill Roulette: Snakes, insects and some ancient animal bones
Notes:
Out into the desert of Namib to master the dunes in the African continent's favourite 4x4. And maybe get stuck a bit too...

Chapter 14

Namibia's dune buggy

The Toyota Land Cruiser has a lot of fans out in the desert of the Namib. If you want to tackle mountain-sized dunes, this is the car to do it in

Words Piers Ward Photography by Steve Perry

'When I breathe out, the air is cooler than when I breathe in. It's harsh for man and machine. The temperature is rising well over 100 degrees'

IT GETS SO HOT HERE THAT when you go to hell you take a blanket with you. It's an old saying in Namibia which I'm beginning to understand. I'm standing at the Orange River camp on the Namibian border with South Africa. When I breathe out, the air is cooler than that I breathed in. It's harsh for man and machine.

That's why Toyota, and specifically the Land Cruiser, has become synonymous with Africa. This machine starts every time and doesn't break.

The very first Land Cruiser pick-up, the true work horse in Namibia, came with a single fuel tank. That was fine for countries like the UK, where you'll only ever go a few miles before another tatty garage forecourt looms into view, no matter how remote the county. But out here, you can be hundreds of miles from anything, let alone fuel. So Namibians fitted their pick-ups with a second fuel tank. Toyota noted this, and made a second tank a standard fit straight away. So now you can get 180 litres in the car. Even the relatively civilised baby Land Cruiser that we get as well, dubbed the Prado in Africa, gets a 180-litre fuel tank. And

you thought the 105 litres you get on a Range Rover was impressive.

Little touches like that have made the Land Cruiser, or 'Cruiser' as the locals seem to prefer, more a way of life than a machine.

In Luderitz I meet Daggie Jahnke, a slip of a woman driving around in an enormous, red 80 Series Cruiser. In Britain, she'd probably be met with disapproving tuts, but in Namibia that doesn't come into the equation. Daggie needs a car that she can regularly drive to Walvis Bay, a trip of 480 miles, over gravel roads and with little other

It takes a special car,
and a special driver,
to scale these dunes

'It's difficult to imagine anywhere
this remote when you're sitting
in your armchair in the UK with a cup of
cocoa and a mobile phone next to you'

Life out here means
you've got to be tough,
not to mention optimistic

passing traffic. Other than her young kids, she's on her own. The Cruiser's never let her down, so why worry?

Everywhere we go, we meet other Land Cruiser owners who would never part with their cars under any circumstances. It's difficult to imagine Africa without this vehicle – it seems to have done more than anything else to mobilise the continent. And with our new-shape 200 Series, I'm not sure we'd have received more attention if we'd been driving a Lamborghini Gallardo.

Everyone wanted to know what it's like, how it drives, how easy it would be to convert to the myriad extra parts that the Namibians seem to come up with for their cars. It's funny, when a Brit first approaches a car, they always cup their hand to the window and look inside. But a Namibian gets down on his or her hands and knees and looks at the suspension. They tap the bumper to see how robust it is. The inside is about the last thing they get to.

We arrive in Bethanie, a frontier town with the temperature nudging 40 degrees, and meet Frans Smit, a local builder who owns a Land Cruiser pick-up. He used to have a Land Rover and his Dad still does, and he freely admits it rides better than his car. But then Frans smiles that slightly nervous smile that seems to mark out Afrikaaners in this part of the world. 'But I still tow him in every so often.'

When you read this, sitting in your armchair with the central heating going, possibly a cup of cocoa beside you, it's difficult to imagine anywhere this remote, given all the world-shrinking technology at our fingertips. But Namibia is nearly the size of Germany and Spain combined, but with only two million inhabitants. Sparse. And when we head into the

Getting beached at the peak of a dune is a constant peril

dunes of the Namib Desert near Luderitz, you begin to appreciate reliability. Mobile phones? Pah! As a minimum you need an HF radio that'll send out a mayday signal.

We're travelling in a three-car convoy. In the dunes, I get stuck time after time because I keep getting beached on top of the 'seesaw', the ridge, and a couple of times the Land Cruiser is belly deep. Our guide, Volker Jahnke, needs to use a couple of firm tugs from his Cruiser pick-up tow-rope to free me. There isn't a cloud in the sky, the Namib Desert has 17 cubic miles of sand in it, I can't see an animal let alone a human, annual rainfall out here is about 20mm – if that Cruiser is properly stuck we're in trouble.

Of course, Volker just keeps smiling, but for a dune virgin like me, things are worrying. Obviously, the reason our Cruiser keeps getting stuck is the clot behind the wheel. I give it too much gas over the top of a dune when I'm not meant to (that translates into one very airborne Land Cruiser), I give it too little at other times and get beached. Volker's constantly on the radio, saying stuff like 'Piers, you must put foot!' when he clears a dune and sees me stuck. Right, get with it,

desert man. Back in Drive, 'put foot' properly this time and plough your way up.

You have no idea what's to come on the other side. All you get is sky above sand, sky above sand, and then – bang

> 'You have no idea what is coming on the other side. All you get is the sky above sand, and then – bang – the nose drops suddenly

– the nose drops suddenly and you're pointing straight down to hell. Well, a very sandy looking hell anyway.

Other than reduced tyre pressure for improved grip in the sand, our Land Cruiser was standard. Volker voiced concerns over the electronics. This guy knows his way around the dunes really well, but 'what happens if keyless go breaks down out here?' The first thing he'd do is take out all the things that beep at you, telling you everything from whether your seatbelt is on, to 'you've left the key in the car' to 'you haven't wiped your backside this morning'. Inconsequential bleepy warnings don't sit well with a desert man and his trusty workhorse.

And you also need to turn every safety device off to get up some of the steeper dunes. The key is momentum, but sometimes little ridges halfway up stop you going hell for leather, or you can't get enough run up. But with all the traction control off, the new Land Cruiser – pretty much the same one that will grace the plethora of school runs of West London in the months to come – will climb anything that Volker's hardcore pick-up will.

The new Cruiser is more effortless, though. Not only does the ride absorb ridges and hillocks (Volker calls them 'little jackals') much better than the other cars in the convoy, but the auto 'box makes light work of driving through the dunes. All that torque and power from the twin-turbo V8 diesel leaves the Hilux for dead on some of the steeper climbs.

In the Sixties, Land Rover was the vehicle for Africa. But now Toyota has conquered it, and it's difficult to see how Land Rover could get a look in. Their new cars simply aren't designed for this territory.

Most importantly, you still get people like Volker sleeping right next to his Cruiser in the desert, waking up in the morning and kissing it fondly. Or people like Carlos dubbing his Toyota a 'waentjie-wa' (ox-wagon) and keeping in touch with the guy who bought his 291,000-miler Hilux. When you see these seriously tough blokes getting soppy and emotional over their cars, you start to realise just what Toyotas mean to them. Out here in the desert, these cars are genuine life-savers.

Er, yes, quite a lot of sand. In fact, mountains of it

Out in this kind of wilderness, you need a reliable car

For sale: fine beach house, panoramic views, light and airy

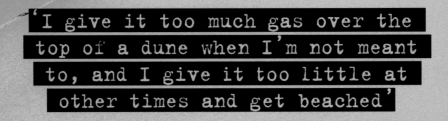

'I give it too much gas over the top of a dune when I'm not meant to, and I give it too little at other times and get beached'

Chapter 15

The rally king of the East

The Fiat 126 Polski is a very special little car, famous for a successful rallying career in Eastern Europe during the late 1970s. Top Gear tracked one of them down

Words Bill Thomas Photography by Steve Perry

THERE HAD TO BE A MOMENT when I saw the Polski Fiat 126 Group 2 for the first time.

It happened as we drove down a narrow road in south-western Poland – there, amid glorious rolling country-side, sitting in front of a neat, red-roofed workshop, was the little blue and white rally car, resplendent in the markings the original wore in the late 1970s, during some of the most heroic drives in rallying history.

This is a car that defies the laws of perspective, because it looks bigger from further away, and gets smaller as you approach. You need to be right up close to appreciate its sensational lack of size – if you've seen a 126 on the road recently, you'll know what I mean. Its lines have aged more gracefully than any 30-year-old car I can think of right now – it's beyond 'cute', it's properly pretty, clean, uncluttered, sweet. If it's small and it's a Fiat, it's hard not to fall in love with.

So I did – I had no choice. I fell in love, at first sight, smitten to the core. And so did *Top Gear* creative director Charlie Turner, another self-confessed small Fiat nut. Only 'nut' can describe a man who would willingly volunteer to accompany me on this 126 drive – a thousand miles from the factory in Poland back to London via Berlin.

You can now buy a 126 replica like this for around £7,000. The cars use original 126 bodyshells and are lovingly prepared by 126 Group 2 in Bielsko Bia_a, just as the old Polish works rally cars were – roll cage, tuned engine, trick suspension, stripped bare. Over three million Polski Fiat 126 road cars were license-built by FSM in Poland between 1973 and 2000, so there are plenty of bodyshells to go round. Polish roads are still clogged with the things. However, to qualify for FIA-spec in historic rallies – the main raison d'être for this replica, though I suspect many people will buy it just to cherish it – the 126 must use a bodyshell constructed between 1978 and 1983.

No problem, thousands to choose from.

It's a little-documented part of rallying history, Poland and Eastern Europe in the late 1970s, but talking to some of the participants and hearing their stories, I can tell you it's at a very high level for sheer guts, bravado and skill. And the FSM-OBR Polski 126s were

POLSKI FIAT

126 Group2 Ex-Works Team

POL

FIAT THROUGH POLAND

Vehicle: Fiat Polski
Climate: Competitive
Distance: 723 miles
Duration: 3 days going sideways
Road Surface: Cobbled and sideways
Roadkill Roulette: Ear drums totally destroyed
Notes:
The Fiat 126 Polski is a forgotten rallying legend. Top Gear tracks it down in Poland and goes for a spin.

POLSKI FIAT

Small on the inside, but this car sure collects some speed

OLSKI FIAT

Driving through some of the picturesque Polish countryside

POLSKI FIAT

in the thick of it, scrapping with far bigger, more powerful cars, and often putting them down.

Andrzej Lubiak, one of the most successful of all the Polski works drivers, met us at the 126 Group 2 factory and told us some tales. I'll never meet a more brilliant raconteur. Andrzej showed us one of his old stage results sheets – and there was his 126, running eighth overall, amongst Renault Alpines and Porsche 911s. Tremendous.

Mounted in the rear, of course, there isn't much between it and the cockpit. It's a two-cylinder, 650cc unit, balanced and blueprinted, with works pistons and cams and a very serious exhaust system. The engine is rated at between 48 and 54bhp depending on its spec – that doesn't sound like much, but the car only weighs 550kg, remember, and 54bhp from 600cc is an exceptional power output. We donned ear defenders and hit the road.

'In one event, rally driver Andrzej Lubiak lost his right front wheel, so his navigator climbed into the rear left corner to keep the nose up'

On one event, he lost a right front wheel – so his navigator climbed onto the left rear corner of the car to keep the nose in the air, then Andrzej finished the stage flat-out. One year he competed in Russia and had to deal with a centimetre of ice inside the windscreen. The demister cleared only a tiny, heart-shaped area in the centre, yet, with his legs wrapped in newspaper, feet clad in ski boots, head bent low to peer through the heart, he carried on at full speed with the temperatures outside at -40°C.

Our first stop would be one of Andrzej's old hunting grounds, the Walim–Ro´sciszów road to the northwest, near the Czech border. Though it was hard to leave the factory, I couldn't wait to try Poland's most famous rally stage in the 126.

Firing up the engine gives you a shock – it is unbelievably loud.

It's a crazy machine to drive. Nothing much happens under 4000rpm, but keep it above that and the 126 zips along briskly – Group 2 engineer Michal Kumiega told us to keep it below 5500, but the tiny twin revs so keenly, it was hard not to let it creep toward the 7,000rpm peak-power point.

Neither Charlie nor I are small people, but we fit inside the 126 without drama. The racing bucket seats in this car are too narrow for my frame, with the side bolsters causing discomfort except when I slid forward, but that was easily fixed. More importantly, though, the driving stance is surprisingly natural given the car's diminutive proportions, with a classic long-arm, short-leg Italian driving position, and the co-pilot's seat set lower and just behind the driver. There's plenty of headroom, too.

Chilling out after a
hard day's drive in
one of Poland's elegant
little towns

Potsdam .... 28 km
Dreieck Nuthetal ... 12 km

Frankfurt (Oder) .. 116 km
Dresden .... 178 km
Berlin-Zentrum ..... 50 km

'It's a crazy machine to drive.
Keep it above 4000rpm and
it zips along briskly and the
engine is unbelievably loud'

The stage near Walim is fabulous, a tight snake across steep forested hills, and the 126 tackled it with élan. This kind of hairpin-infested road is what the 126 is made for, especially with the optional short-ratio gearbox fitted to our test car – its 18kph per thousand revs in top (fourth) didn't really make much sense on fast A-roads, but here it was perfect. The trick is to keep

Fiat into a truck.

Heading through Berlin the next morning, we blasted pedestrians and other motorists with deafening engine blips before parking the 126 at the Brandenburg Gate for a photo. Surely no car in the world has such a massive sound-to-size ratio, and judging by the reaction of everyone who set eyes on it, there can't be many more attractive cars in existence, either.

> ## 'Surely no other car in the world has such a massive sound-to-size ratio. And there can't be many more attractive cars around either'

your momentum up at all costs, and keep the revs up with it. That's a lot of fun, because the 126 turns in with great precision and holds its line with proper determination – the 165/55 Yokohama 12-inch tyres don't want to let go, and you can adjust the tail with a little lift when the car is at the limit of adhesion. Held tight by the racing seats, dialling in the lock with the Monte Carlo steering wheel and keeping the revs high with constant use of the quick, easy-shifting 'box, it's not hard to imagine master drivers like Andrzej embarrassing those pesky Alpines.

I'd like to say that we drove the 126 all the way to Berlin, our overnight stop, in a marathon endurance run, but that would be a bare-faced lie. The short-ratio 'box meant that 60mph equalled 5,500rpm and it wasn't fair on the car. We slid the little

We then did a long stint on a mostly derestricted autobahn, sitting at 60mph and dicing with trucks. As big Mercs and Audis piled past, the 126 rocked on its little wheels and I quietly dreamt of leaving the exec-mobiles behind on a switchback road. If you're thinking of tackling longer journeys with this car, I'd recommend you get the longer-ratio 'box option, where a top speed of 90mph makes a lot more sense.

'Sense' isn't a word you'd normally associate with a rally replica, but maybe the guys at Group 2 are onto something here – this is a car that works brilliantly in the world we find ourselves in. Tiny, nimble, charismatic, inexpensive to buy and run, and above all, a gigantic dollop of unmitigated fun – you can sit in it and flick the bird at the world. Then, when you step out, you'll turn to look at it and it feels like the first time.

Chapter 16

The pearl of the Orient

The pearl being the Ferrari 612 Scaglietti and this bit of the Orient being the 21st century powerhouse, China. Will the Chinese take to its charms? Just a bit

Words Alistair Weaver Photography by Anton Watts

FERRARI IN CHINA

Vehicle: Ferrari 612 Scaglietti
Climate: Smoggy
Distance: 1464 miles
Duration: 8 days and 7 nights
Road Surface: Lots of gravel traps
Roadkill Roulette: Anyone driving on the wrong side of the road
Notes:
Far to the west of Beijing, the Chinese border to Afghanistan makes for a different way to experience this vast country.

road along which silk and medicine travelled west, while wool, glass and vegetables flowed east.

I meet 'Red Squadron' at Kashi, a town at odds with the perceived image of developing China. Geographically closer to Europe than it is to Beijing, Kashi is just 200 miles from the Afghanistan border on the western edge of China. The people here speak Turkic, not Chinese, and Islam is still widely followed.

Officially, this area is known as the Xinjiang Uighur Autonomous Region, but the extent of this 'autonomy' is open to debate. The Communist Party annexed this region 55 years ago and

The Ferrari turns everyone around it into the paparazzi

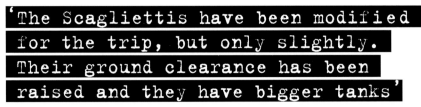

'The Scagliettis have been modified for the trip, but only slightly. Their ground clearance has been raised and they have bigger tanks'

'WE ARE THE RED SQUADRON,' says Luigino 'Gigi' Barp, Ferrari's After Sales Director. 'We have clear rules and strict discipline. People must know and trust the boss – me.'

For Barp, who was previously a test engineer in the Italian air force, Ferrari's '15,000 Red Miles' isn't just a PR stunt or even an epic expedition; it's virtually a military operation. Ever since two 612 Scagliettis left Beijing on 29 August, he has been given command of seven vehicles and 17 people in an attempt to cross some of the least hospitable parts of China.

It's 4 October, and there are still 5,300 miles to go before the cars are due to arrive in Shanghai on 29 October. For the next week, I will join 'Red Squadron' as it tracks east along the Silk Road, the old trading route between east and west. In medieval times, this route was the commercial

instigated a dramatic process of 'sinification', which included the mass immigration of up to seven million Han Chinese. The teaching of Islam is banned in schools and a 'Great Western Development Plan' to improve the standard of living has met a mixed response from the Uighur people.

Not surprisingly then, the Chinese authorities were reluctant to allow Ferrari to use such regions in this exercise. Even Ferrari is willing to admit the tour is a public relations stunt, designed to generate exposure for a company that doesn't employ traditional advertising techniques.

'Our original proposal for a tour of China was rejected,' says Ferrari's PR guru, Antonio Ghini. 'But by repackaging the tour as a sporting event, we were able to gain the support of the Ministry for Sport.' Without this, the trip would've been unthinkable.

'Excuse me little one, but is this the right way to go to the Sea of Death?'

'In near-zero visibility we push on, relying on our

reflexes and the strength of the 612's suspension'

We roll out of Kashi at 8.30am, when it's still dark. Despite its location, Xinjiang adheres to Beijing time. Its residents therefore live in a bizarre world in which it doesn't get light until mid-morning and darkness arrives late in the evening.

The roads are surprisingly good and we settle into an easy, 80mph cruise. The Scagliettis have been modified for the trip, but only very slightly. Their ground clearance has been raised by 100mm and cladding guards their underbodies. The fuel tanks are 45 litres larger than standard, the headlights boast a protective grille and snow tyres do battle with the desert sand.

Our squadron consists of seven vehicles – two Fiat Palios, two Ferraris,

Although we're well equipped with spares, we've no means of repairing a crashed Ferrari and the only spare car is 2,000 miles away in Shanghai. To bin it now, two-thirds of the way through the journey, would be to incur the wrath of the Italian nation.

My fears are compounded by the Chinese driving standards. The highways are not so much roads, as strips of ground upon which the locals see fit to travel. Officially, you drive on the right in China, but no one seems to care. It's not unusual to find a horse and cart trundling towards you on the wrong side of the road; motorbikes scurry every which way and no one stops at a junction.

By the end of the second day, we arrive in the small town of Minfeng,

'You're going to drive on these roads in that? The kids see the funny side

'Officially you drive on the right in China, but no one seems to care. It's not unusual to find a horse and cart driving straight at you'

two minibuses and an Iveco army truck packed with spare parts. There are also 13 support staff including two engineers from Maranello: Silvano Baldini is in charge of the bodywork and suspension, while Renato Bonettini has to keep the electronics in order. Seven of the party are Chinese nationals, including Xie Xiao, the government official who is also our tour guide.

Barp spends most of his time at the front of our convoy in a Palio, relaying information about the road ahead, and its value is proven when the highway suddenly comes to an end. We're diverted off-road onto a rough gravel track that would trouble an SUV. I slow to a crawl and cringe as the harsh desert rocks do battle with the 612's protective cladding.

'Give me a motorbike
any day of the week,'
argues one resident

On the northern edge of the desert, we find its hidden treasure. A Sinopec installation sucks oil from the desert floor, driving China's economic renaissance. This area is rich in natural resources, which is why the Xinjiang province remains so important to Beijing. A makeshift village serves the workforce and, as we head east towards Jiayuguan, we encounter even more 'nomadic' communities, which service the railroad and highway construction.

In near-zero visibility we push on, relying on our reflexes and the strength of the 612's suspension. The prancing horse on the steering wheel bucks uneasily in my hand as we play chicken with the overloaded trucks that prowl the highway. There is little time for reflection – the clock is ticking and the thought of tackling such terrain in the dark is nothing short of horrifying. A wheel rim on the silver car eventually cries enough, but with the exception of a pause to clean an air filter in the desert, this is the only time in six days that we've been forced to stop.

The road finally improves again as the city of Jiayuguan appears on the horizon. We're in the Gansu province, beyond the Tarim Basin. Historically referred to as the 'mouth' of China, it holds a symbolic location at the end of the Great Wall. On the final day we pay homage to this epic construction which is a symbol of China old and new.

It would be easy to dismiss Ferrari's '15,000 Red Miles' as a token PR stunt. But to be unduly cynical is to be dismissive of an impressive achievement. Securing the support of the Chinese government and then completing a journey that took two Ferraris through some of the world's most inhospitable scenery was a fine effort. Stunt or not, this is one expedition to the harsh regions of Southeast Asia that could be hailed as a genuine success.

on the edge of the Taklimakan desert. The town has a busy high street, packed with market stalls and cafes.

I park the Ferrari, which soon draws a crowd. The locals peer through the windows, circle it nosily and grab at the door handles. The town is poor, which makes the sight of a £170,500 supercar all the more incongruous.

Through a translator, I snatch a word with one of the spectators, Uquili. He claims to have seen a Grand Prix on television, but has no knowledge of Ferrari's road cars. 'I have no money,' he says, 'but I am confident that in the future I will afford a car.' His words are echoed by others we meet along the way. China is going through an epic period of change, and through the dust and rubble it's possible to discern a definite current of optimism.

Next morning, we leave Minfeng and head north, across the desert. Covering an area of more than 130,000sq miles, the Taklimakan is the second largest in the world. The locals call it the 'Sea of Death' and it's easy to see why. While the natural beauty of the dunes is undeniable, it's difficult to think of a more inhospitable environment.

'The Ferrari soon draws a crowd. The locals peer through the windows, circle it noisily and grab at the door handles'

JPN

THE iCAR IN JAPAN

Vehicle: Mitsubishi iCar
Climate: Suffocating
Distance: 709 miles
Duration: 4 claustrophobic nights
Road Surface: Perfect tarmac
Roadkill Roulette: In something this size, we're the roadkill
Notes:
An honourable journey to the land of the rising sun, to sample the iCar in its natural environment and experience a capsule hotel.

Chapter 17

It's a small world out there

In Japan, a country that does small on a very big scale, what better way to get to grips with the culture than by using a small car and small hotels. Very small hotels

Words Bill Thomas Photography by Tom Salt

'What the polite woman would never say, but what is heavily implied, is that capsule hotels are stinking male-only doss houses for drunks'

THE GIRL AT MITSUBISHI IN Japan could not have been more professional and polite when she helped us organise this story. She dealt with us in perfect English, arranged the loan of the iCar with efficiency, everything was beautifully done. But the accommodation we asked her to book was a cause for concern. Here's how she expressed it in an email:

'I booked the hotel according to the request, but could you make sure whether the capsule hotels are really OK with them? Because it is very affordable but the way

of room is quite unique and small like single bed size.'

'Very affordable' means 2,300 yen per night, or about £10. 'Small like single bed size' means the whole room, not just the bed. And 'way of room is quite unique' means 'don't do it, you're insane, you have no idea what you're getting yourselves into'.

'The way of room is quite unique'. Ah, the politeness of that mild, but heartfelt warning. What the helpful girl from Mitsubishi would never say, but what is heavily implied, is that capsule hotels are stinking, smoke-

ridden, male-only dosshouses for drunks and semi-bums, the last desperate act for when you've had a few too many sakes and need to crash somewhere, anywhere, for the night.

A Japanese friend of mine, who is a little more forthright than most of his countrymen, explained it like this, and winced when he said it: 'How best to say? [Wince] Capsule hotel is a little bit for lower-class people. You and I would stay in normal-style hotel, not this capsule place.'

Still, this drive story needs to be done properly, despite the warnings.

Fine for sleeping.
Just don't try to
stand up in there

Tiny Japanese car, tiny Japanese rooms, and the four biggest Japanese cities in order over 500 miles – Osaka, Nagoya, Yokohama, Tokyo. But when I set eyes on my first capsule, I wasn't sure it'd be worth it. One look at that plastic coffin and the extremeness of Japan gripped me like a sumo's death-hold.

The flight landed in Osaka early on a Tuesday morning. Tom Salt and I picked up the i, set its Japanese-only satnav system by programming in the capsule hotel's phone number, and drove straight there in the bright sunshine to the sound of a high-pitched female voice barking 'hidare-ho-ho' and 'migi-ho-ho' constantly. Luckily, hidare (left) and migi (right) are two of the Japanese words I know, along with arigato (thanks), sayonara (bye) and mawashi hijiate (roundhouse elbow smash).

The Osaka capsule hotel is the oldest in the world – located on the top floor of a nondescript beige building in a seedy part of town, surrounded by places with names like 'Joy Palace' and 'Soap World Plus'. The whole area was being hosed down. We arrived at reception and immediately started breaking protocol by asking whether we could inspect the 'rooms' and dump our gear in them. You're supposed to leave your bags in lockers near reception and change into robes before going anywhere near the capsules, but we didn't know any of that and we didn't ask. All we managed to do by way of protocol was remove our shoes.

No other guests were there at 11am, of course – just a well-drilled, military-style team of cleaners wearing thick masks and even thicker gloves. Despite their near-nuclear-strength cleaning fluids, the place stank of cigarette ash and something older and

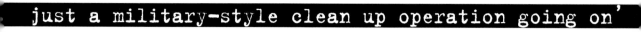

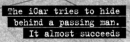
The iCar tries to hide behind a passing man. It almost succeeds

deeper, an indefinable, ancient, nasty sweetness. Some of the odour came from the carpets – dark brown thick shag pile and 30 years old if they were a day, which you'd expect in the oldest capsule hotel in the world. But some of the odour came from elsewhere. It was an evil, all-pervading semi-fishy smell and I didn't like it.

Oh Jesus, no, I'm not sleeping in that. My 'room' was at the top of a double row of 12, accessible by a set of ladder steps that you could easily twist an ankle on, especially if you were drunk. I leapt in and immediately cracked my knee on the hard plastic beneath the mattress, which is little more than a blanket, about an inch thick. At the far end of the capsule was a light and an industrial-looking ventilation swivel nozzle that seemed black with grime inside. It blasted air into the capsule with a steady roar, and I wondered how many old smog-lined pipes and ducts were touched by the bit of air I was sucking in. I hopped right to the back, bashing my head as I did so, and immediately felt the wipe-clean beige plastic walls closing in around me.

I'm not claustrophobic, but I understand the condition better now. Distraction, please, I need a distraction. Look at these controls for radio, TV and lights, wow – they're Seventies-era toggles, Space 1999-style, unchanged since the place first opened. Next to the ceiling-mounted colour TV was a coin box for Y100 pieces. Y100 is about 50p and pays for 10 hours of porn, so I'm told.

We staggered out of there and went for a drive around Osaka. It is a spectacular city of 19 million when you include adjoining Kobe and Kyoto, defined by a tremendous number of fantastic bridges crossing myriad waterways and leading to one of the world's most dramatic ports. We

Roadways that loop like ribbons in the sky. Very Japanese

found an expressway that headed straight into the sky and turned right. We went to a dockside area beneath an otherworldly spiral of motorway flyovers. And wherever we stopped to take pictures, the Japanese were polite and helpful and never interfered. They were highly amused that we were driving such a tiny car on Tokyo plates, because they assumed we had driven it from there. When we got to Tokyo, we made sure everyone knew we'd driven it from Osaka. My, oh how we all laughed.

After our photosession, we parked the i near the hotel and for the first time ever on a driving trip, I looked back at a car and envied it as a form of accommodation. The i would be spacious, with a soft bed, and windows. Photographer Salt and I made dinner last as long as possible, and it wasn't long before the word 'violate' came up in conversation. My violation nightmare was a drunk sumo-sized frenzied gay ultra-violent western-man-loving freak jamming himself into my pod but being too big to fit, plugging the opening and roaring at me and waving his arms and trying to grab my legs and do nasty things to me. Tom was worried about real issues like fires and earthquakes and about the noises he might hear during the night – the

regular clattering of coins into slots and other sounds not mentionable in a family magazine.

After donning our gowns and avoiding the communal lounge, which was populated by heavy smokers, all staggering around drunk, we hit the 'sack'. A little blind pulls down to separate you from the corridor and mine had holes in it – there is no privacy. The pod was not comfortable, either – the pillow felt like it was stuffed with walnuts and the blast from the ventilation nozzle was loud. Even jet-lagged to hell after missing a night and having been awake for 36 hours, I didn't sleep a wink in that capsule before the alarm went off at 7am. Up we get, then. Let's drive to Nagoya.

The little Mitsubishi i is very good indeed – funky, charming, amazingly spacious and practical, and on sale in the UK now for £8,999. As we headed out of Osaka toward Kyoto, the i needed to be easy to drive and com-

fortable in the rotten post-capsule state I was in – and it was. It makes a Smart look like yesterday's car and Mitsubishi UK will sell as many as it can import.

The i is designated a Kei Car (or K-Car) in Japan, a category that wears black-on-yellow plates, that must comply with strict width and length restrictions and, unlike 'normal' white plate cars, that doesn't need its own dedicated parking spot by law. The Japanese K-Car market was one million units large last year, dominated by the square-box Daihatsu Move, which is under fire from all quarters. Other K's include the Subaru R1 coupe, Daihatsu Copen roadster and – Google this one, it's great – the Honda Vamos mini truck. The i will take a large share because it looks funkier than any of them.

> '**After donning our gowns and avoiding the lounge populated by heavy smokers, all staggering around drunk, we hit the sack**'

The engine is a three-cylinder 659cc DOHC turbo, mounted under the floor of the boot, driving the rear wheels through a standard four-speed automatic gearbox. The latter is an excellent idea – forget the nastiness of Smart's semi-manual set-up. At 63bhp it's obviously not a fast car, but it'll still surprise you when you give it full beans and it runs easily on the motorway up to its limited top speed of 140kmh (87mph).

It is surprisingly spacious, thanks to an extremely long wheelbase which pushes the front wheelarches beyond the nose. It's a comfortable and capable city car and it did us proud as we travelled to Nagoya via the coast road.

Japan isn't only
about the little
things, you know

Here we discovered that Japan isn't all about bustling cities and traffic jams and enclosed spaces. In fact, we got a taste of exactly what Japan is all about – tranquil, spectacular coastlines and mountains. The feeling of peace and vast open space around Kumano and Shingu was a great tonic for the cramped lodging we'd just experienced – and what we were heading for next.

More capsuleness awaited us in Nagoya, but this time we felt experienced and worldly-wise when it came to checking in. We were now officially capsule hotel professionals and everything was familiar and natural. As in Osaka, the staff were extremely surprised to discover that we had a reservation. We put our shoes in a small locker in reception, received our locker key, which was provided with a plastic wrist strap, dumped our gear in the locker and donned the light-blue prison-style pyjamas supplied.

In case you ever want to try one, the trick with making a stay in a capsule hotel bearable is to make full use of the facilities. In the case of the Nagoya Capsule Inn, and most others like it, an elaborate spa was on the floor below. For a small extra cost, you could make use of saunas, showers and a large communal steam room and bath area. I did it all, stripping off and enjoying a traditional-style Japanese bath, complete with a very small chair, a rock-solid piece of soap and a bucket to pour water over yourself. I felt like a large and hairy white whale as I wandered around the facilities among much smaller gents, and half expected one of the guys in there to point a spear gun at me and harpoon me for blubber.

Having relaxed in the spa and sauna, and having been awake for 56 straight hours, sleep came easily in Nagoya capsule number 3107. I was woken only once, at about 3am, by some loud and bitter laughter outside my pod. I don't know what was funny and I really didn't wish to find out.

Day three dawned bright and sunny, and the first thing I did was put diesel in the car. That would have been fine if it had had a diesel engine. I knew it was a petrol engine, but the choices facing me at the pump weren't easy. There was a green, a red and a black nozzle, with no English markings in sight. The red I thought might be four-star. Don't know why I thought that. The black I thought might be diesel, because black is diesel where I come from. So green it was. Green for safety. Green means go. In with the green nozzle. With no attendants around to help, green it was. I didn't bother sniffing it first, because, well, I'm an idiot.

We got 100 yards down the road before the little i coughed and died.

> **'In Nagoya we discovered that Japan isn't about bustling cities and traffic jams. We got a taste of what it is all about – tranquil, spectacular coastlines and mountains'**

So, half an hour later, we met the JAF man. JAF is the Japanese AA and the old guy in the truck was perfectly happy and helpful, wearing his JAF cap proudly. He spoke not a word of English, except one – when I showed him the fuel receipt, he drew a circle around whatever kanji characters indicated diesel, then looked up at me and said, very clearly, 'mistake'.

Mistake indeed. The fuel tank had to come off at the local Mitsubishi dealer, and the system had to be drained. Looking at the underside of the car was interesting – it is brilliantly packaged, with the engine slotted neatly behind the rear axle and the tank ahead of it, with tubes running from the front-mounted radiator. Amazing how they can slot everything in and still leave room for four adults and quite a bit of luggage. What a great little car.

Replenished with the right fuel, the run into Tokyo was relatively straightforward. We planned to take some shots around Mount Fuji, but it was invisible, covered in haze. Traffic is never as bad in Japan as people make out, and before long our friendly Japanese satnav girl had *migi*'d and *hidare*'d us along the Shuto expressway and into the heart of the world's largest city.

Tired and a bit miserable, facing a 7am check-in the next morning at Narita Airport, an hour's drive from Tokyo centre, we pulled up outside our 'hotel' in Akihabara. As usual, the 'capsule place' was in a nondescript beige building marked with a picture of a little man sleeping in a tube. Tonight, I didn't want to be that man. After between five and 15 seconds of discussion, I rang the Radisson.

We were supposed to drop the icar back to Mitsubishi that evening, but it never happened. I put the car straight up to its maximum speed and made a beeline for the Radisson Narita. Checking in to that hotel was one of the most pleasant things I have ever done.

Ah, the wonder of it! You'll never properly appreciate a normal room with a normal bed unless you spend a couple of nights in a capsule. 'Unique' just isn't the word for the way of capsule room.

ARC

ATOM TO THE ARCTIC

Vehicle: Ariel Atom
Climate: Breezy
Distance: 1137 miles
Duration: 6 cold days and nights
Road Surface: A tad slippery
Roadkill Roulette: Lots of polar bears. No, only kidding!
Notes:
For reasons that owe a lot to insanity, the plan is to get some scaffolding on wheels into the Arctic Circle. And not die doing it.

Arctic Circle

Chapter 18

Welcome to life in the freezer

An Ariel Atom is a car that you might describe as being a little 'exposed'. It's also a bit tricky to handle. So one place you really shouldn't take it is the Arctic. Er...

Words Tom Ford Photography by Lee Brimble

90

E 6

going to make the 1,000-miles to the Arctic Circle. Not in an Ariel Atom. Not at this time of year.

It all seemed so easy from the comfortable refuge of four pints of cider. We would spend a few days driving to the Arctic Circle in a car quite obviously not designed to do so. Like an Ariel Atom. We would wrap up warm, take some nice pictures and be home in time for tea and sticky-buttered crumpets.

Fuelled on thoughts of *Boy's Own*-style adventure, we sallied forth to Newcastle for the 19-hour ferry trip to Kristiansand on the southern edge of Norway, planning to be back within a

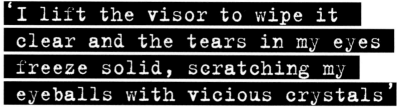

'I lift the visor to wipe it clear and the tears in my eyes freeze solid, scratching my eyeballs with vicious crystals'

It isn't long before madness starts to set in

I AM FROZEN MEAT. MY WEAK, temperate circulation waved the white flag some 30 feet from Norwegian customs, and at 60 feet I couldn't feel my feet. An hour in, my hands might as well be plastic.

My senses seem to be a bit muddled, because at one point I swear that my feet are bleeding; that my boots are full of blood. I try not to think about it and desperately mumble a confused version of Captain Sensible's 'Happy Talk' into my helmet while ice clogs the inside of my visor. Lifting the plastic to wipe it clear, the tears in my eyes freeze solid, scratching my eyeballs with unforgiving, vicious little crystals. My nose hair stiffens, my lips crack, and a stray lock of slightly sweaty hair sets solid, flash-frozen. Fifty miles in, I whimperingly pull over to discuss the trip with the support crew in the Land Rover. We are, quite patently, not

few days. We were attracting plenty of interest wherever we stopped, especially when we rocked up at the Royal Docks and encountered real Norwegians. At first we laughed at the little sucking noises they made through their teeth. The twisted-up purse of the lips that signified both incredulity and the prospect of reading about us in the local newspaper. People kept looking at me with the kind of sad, remorseful look you might expect if you told someone you had a terminal disease. 'Oh dear', said their eyes, 'how awful for you'. Extravagantly mustachioed Norwegian men strode up to the car, inspected the blatantly stud-less tyres and announced: 'You are doing this? In that? Now? You are crazy! No, actually, I think you are stupid.' We laughed, with only a slight edge. It wasn't so bad, was it? The trip to Newcastle had been OK, to be honest.

'It's not a speeding ticket, sir. I'm writing out a form to have you sectioned under the mental health act'

'The whole trip had seemed so easy from the warm and

comfortable refuge of four pints of cider in a pub'

Twenty-one hours later, we're checking the return ferry times and trying to think of a plausible excuse for only getting as far as Oslo. It doesn't help. We have to keep going, at least for a bit. Have to try. It's hard though; the Ariel slips, scrabbles and spins along roads composed solely of sheet ice and snowy fluff as lorries stamp quickly past on studded tyres. A two-hour stint feels as if you've been battered senseless, and fingers become randomly, painfully numb. Toes. I remember toes.

The countryside is a dirty blizzard of white, nothing to see except dual carriageway and the occasional Colgate-white shock of sunlight. There is no distance view. Thinking slows, brains take longer to engage

sitting in the full blast of an Atom's bare frontage, you're looking at a continuous -55.

Confusingly, Trondheim doesn't look too far away on a large-scale map, and, as dawn breaks bright and clear, we step on up the E6 towards it with hope in our hearts. We've discovered shorter stints in the Atom, followed by periods with our feet stuffed into the Landie's rear heater vents might be a way of preventing ourselves being referred to as 'Stumpy' in the pub, post-trip. And it helps that, as the roads slowly degrade into shiny pistes, the views pull their socks up, encouraging us around the next bend. Suddenly, the Atom feels small and fragile in a country that has no time for the comforts of summer.

It's liable to a bit of wheelspin in these conditions

'We have to keep going. Have to try. It's hard though; the Ariel slips, scrabbles and spins along roads composed entirely of sheet ice'

and hatred for the evil bastards in the warm Land Rover festers.

The temperature, according to the Discovery's gauge, is dropping to -10. Heat pads are stuffed into gloves and boots, two balaclavas are worn under helmets and still we freeze. The chill oils itself through the gloves and boots and creeps up arms and legs.

We reach Oslo the first night and decide not to turn back quite yet because we aren't quitters. Some backslapping occurs for getting this far, and we think seriously about lying about getting there. We decide not to, and it proves to be yet another bookmark in our litany of daft. Overnight, the temperature drops to -32 and both headlights on the Atom shatter in the cold – and that's without wind chill; with it, at 60mph,

'Two-and-a-half hours later, I see the sign. The Arctic Circle sign. And I cross it, in an Ariel Atom, in winter. Bloody hell, we made it'

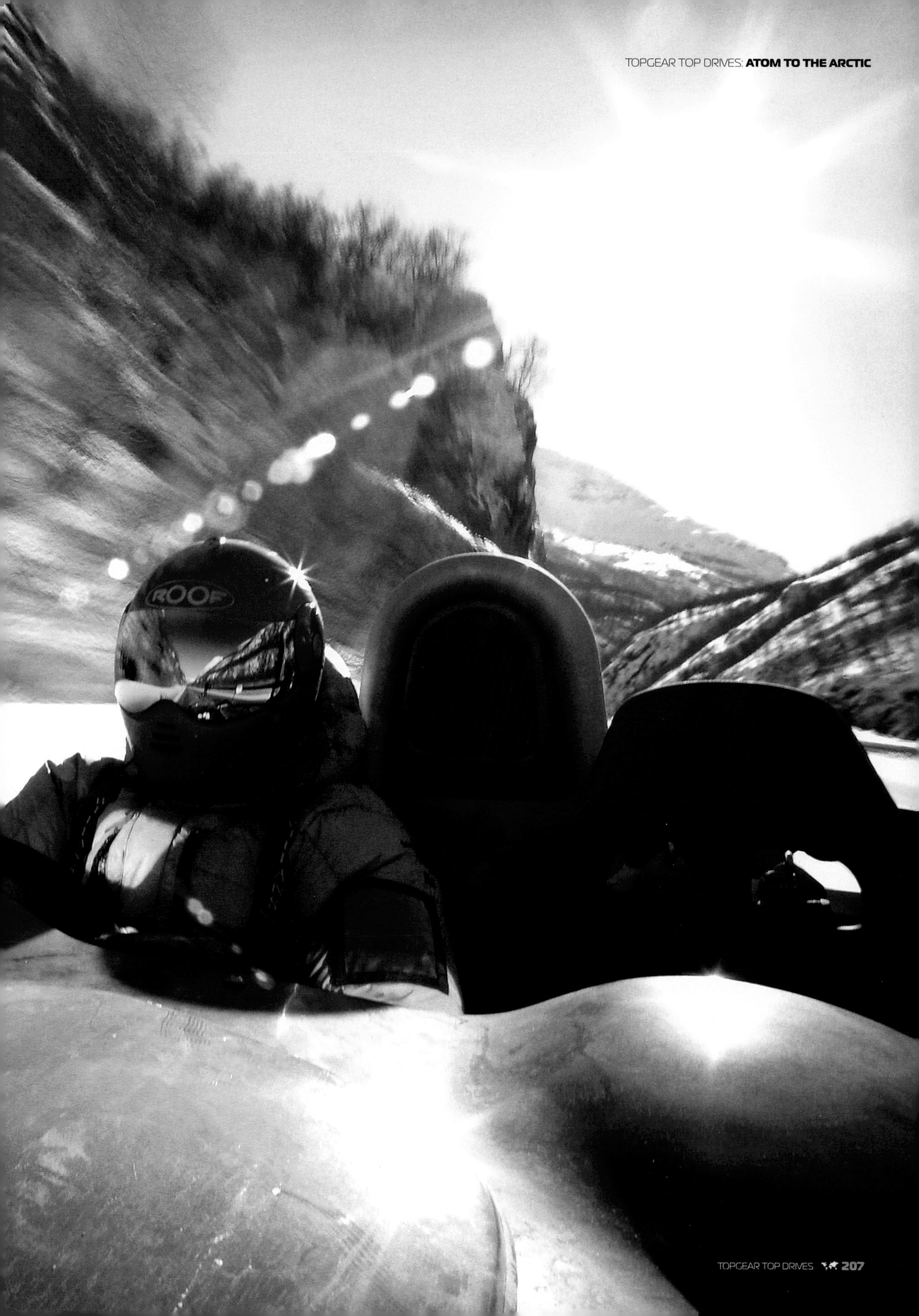
ROOF

to go a bit pear-shaped as we enter a tunnel, mainly because I see a chance to overtake. Halfway down, and on the wrong side of the road, I hit black ice and start to slide. Puckering every orifice, I flail from full left lock to full right lock, losing speed all the time, before clipping the rear mudguard of the lorry with the front wing of the Atom and spinning clear. For what seemed like forever all I could see was unfeeling, grinding lorry wheel.

Four hours later and the blackness is total. No street lights, no stars. The Circle does not exist on the Land Rover's satnav, and what we thought to be 20 miles is, in fact, 50. We're still 50 miles away. Another two hours. My sense of humour fails, I scream, shout, cry like a baby. Throw my helmet on the floor. I must cross the line myself. Tonight. But I'm bloody hurting, or I would be, if I could feel anything in my lumpen limbs.

Two-and-a-half hours later, I see the sign. The Arctic Circle sign. And I cross it, in an Atom, in winter. Bloody hell, we made it.

With little energy left to congratulate each other, we stay at a little truckers' guest house nearby and in the morning trek back up to the Circle to see what we missed in the dark. No trees, no houses, nothing. You enter the tundra, and the desolation is complete. But it's also incredibly beautiful. The two posts that mark the Arctic Circle's path are the only landmarks, the rest a waveform of white. The superlatives dry up and we're reduced to wandering around mouthing 'wow' at each other like senile goldfish.

An hour of taking in the view later, and we point the cars south, ready for the return slog. It has been a vivid thing, this drive. But the only way I'm ever going to do something as daft as this again is if Hell freezes over.

'Damn, I forgot to pack that thermal underwear. Oh well.'

We stop in a garage at the side of the road, and fall into bed exhausted at 9pm, just past Trondheim. It feels as if we've been going for three weeks. It's been three days.

I wake up to find one of the crew phoning the ferry company. We've already missed our boat home, and the next one isn't until Sunday, so we might as well keep going as far as we can. The next stop is, potentially, a place called Mo-I-Rana, some 20 miles short of the Circle. We don't really expect to get there, but the roads seem good so we start early. Soon we're down to 25mph, the Ariel reduced to a crawl along a slick line of glass-ice between two walls of snow.

Eventually, after too many hours of driving, it becomes clear that if we put in the hours and take our time we might just make it. We're 100 miles from Mo-I-Rana, about 120 miles from the Circle and it's late afternoon. We decide to make a break for it and try to beat the impending weather. I take the wheel, start following one of the many lorries tracking their non-stop way up the mountains. It all starts

The Atom makes it
to the Arctic Circle.
How, we'll never know

Chapter 19

In deep trouble in Canada

Head out to northern Canada in the middle of winter and you'll find a unique road, one that disappears when summer arrives. The perfect place to take a Jeep

Words Tom Ford Photography by Barry Hayden

<CNA

THE CANADIAN ICE ROAD

Vehicle: Jeep Commander
Climate: About to crack
Distance: 142 miles
Duration: 3 days and nights
Road Surface: Dirt track
Roadkill Roulette: Stuffed dog,
stuffed deer, stuffed bear...
Notes:
It's a road that can only be
traversed in winter, in one of
the most remote parts of the world.
Welcome to the Canadian wilderness.

To take my mind off madman's mad eyes, I take a quick scan around the room. Taxidermy looks to be a popular hobby around these parts, and judging by the state of the various wall-mounted exhibits, it is practised mainly while drunk, with Grubby Cap getting a pre-emptive human embalming via the toxic medium of the local hooch. I feel like I'm a very long way from home.

Which, to be fair, I am. 'These parts' are Eagle Plains (population: a throbbing, party-making 8), 'kilometres 371' on the Dempster Highway in Canada's Yukon. Flying several hours north of Vancouver in a tin sheet and pop-riveted aeroplane (or a couple of long

Just remember to keep on all those traction controls

> 'Remote is a good word to use about places on the Dempster highway. Another is cold. It claws the skin with little white rodent talons'

'YOU'RE BETTER OFF KICKING a bear in the ass and running away, than seeing one of those things from a mile off,' says a man in a grubby trucker's cap from two tables over. 'Even the old trappers stay away from the wolverines. They'll take the damn tyres off your car.'

'Uh, OK,' I say, somewhat unsure of how to reply to this wildly exaggerated statement about a stuffed carcass that looks like an unhappy cross between a badger and a steroid-addicted pine marten. 'It doesn't look that bad,' I say, trying to be polite without actually initiating a full conversation, 'a bit, er, unhappy.'

Grubby Cap stares at me like I've just tried to get amorous with his dog. It wouldn't be so bad, but as his left eye locks onto mine, the other is oscillating wildly trying to get a lock on something three feet over my left shoulder.

days in a car) gets you here and, using this as a jump-off, you can motor fairly easily along to the Northwest Territories and past the Arctic Circle, eventually ending your journey – if you're not really paying attention – with a plop which signifies the Arctic Ocean.

The reason there are so few souls to engage in wolverine-related conversation is that 'remote' is a good word to use about the places on the Dempster – especially in winter. Another one is cold. People don't get up here much when the weather closes in at -25 ambient (-50 with wind chill factored in). It's the kind of cold that claws into skin with little white rodent talons and won't let go. Where the mucus in your nose freezes; where the first deep breath makes you cough, as your lungs attempt to shock away air that feels like it's the temperature of liquid nitrogen. Suck -30 through your teeth and they

Here's looking at you. Now isn't it about time you opened that can of dog meat?

'We're here not just to drive on the most northerly

'road in the world, but one that isn't a road at all'

 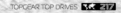

tick, nearly crack with the extreme contraction. It seems a strange place to come for fun.

The reason we're here isn't just to drive the third most northerly public highway in the world, which the Dempster is, (though that's pretty impressive in itself), but to drive a very special road that isn't a road. Because it's a river. And an ocean. And we've not come mounted in the GT version of some military Argocat – we've come in standard Jeep Commanders without winter tyres. So far I haven't seen any secret under-body floats or a button marked 'hover', so I'm hoping my other information is on the money.

It works like this: drive north a few hundred miles from Eagle Plains, where Mr G. Cap carves out a living stuffing dead things, and you come to a place called Inuvik. Now Inuvik is more or less where the local Inuvaluit people (the ethnically correct version of 'Inuit') consider to be the southern border. Truck on out of Inuvik in the summer and you're likely to drown. To get to the next town of Tuktoyaktuk ('Tuk' for short) on the edge of the Arctic Ocean, you'll need a boat, or an aeroplane with floats on. In the winter, however, you can drive to Tuk on a frozen river, and subsequently on an equally frigid bit of the Arctic Ocean.

Bizarrely, this isn't some expedition-spec specialist undertaking. You can do it in a relatively normal car. And get this: because the road is inspected by the proper authorities (meeting the requisite 150ft width requirements and safety regs), it's actually classified as a proper Canadian highway.

Your insurance is valid (unless you go from April to September, in which case you need to contact the maritime people and have an engine with

'Mercury' or 'Evinrude' printed on the side), your car is safe(-ish) and you can say that you've driven on water for hundreds of miles like some 21st-century automotive Jesus going for a ramble on B-roads carved out of the Sea of Galilee. Albeit water that's frozen solid – six feet deep.

OK, so four-wheel drive and some ground clearance is more than preferable, simply because the ice can get pretty lumpy and if you do slide off into a snow bank, you want to give yourself the best chance of not ending up as a novelty icicle. But in theory, you could do this in the very SUV you drive around town. The Commander is the perfect choice, simply because this is what Jeep people imagine themselves doing on their days off, even if they never do.

Unfortunately for Jeep – and much in the same vein as every other 4x4 maker out there – it has to guarantee that the Commander has all the bits to make sure that it can mountaineer, just so that the 0.1 per cent of people that do actually try going off-road don't implode with self-righteous anger and company writs.

The new Commander, therefore, has all the right stripes and credentials rufty-tufty-wise. It even looks like it's trying to be encouraging – all exposed hex-bolts on the arches and tough-looking, semi-military lines. 'Hey!' it says, 'I'm ready when you are! Bring on the wilderness! Let's go have an adventure!'. It's dying to show off its Quadra-Trac II electronic diffs and super-dooper 4x4. Having driven hundreds of miles on ice roads with all the electronics switched on and not even a hint of wobble, I laugh in the face of Jeep's engineers and switch everything off the first proper chance I get. My skill rather than silicon guard dogs any day, that's how I see it.

Ice warms up the tyres, but snow cools them down. Easy life, then

Just like life in Croydon. Except with more animal skins on the line

Within 30 seconds I'm slithering gracelessly across the road, then off it, then into the three-foot deep snow on the edge of the ludicrously cambered road. 'Stuck' would be a very light-hearted way of putting it. Luckily, there are three Jeeps in our convoy capable of a snatch recovery, or I could have spent a very disturbing night sharing my body heat with Barry the photographer. Lesson learned, the button stays unpushed until there's a whole lot more space to play in.

Still, onwards and upwards from Eagle Plains we go, through alumini-um towns with houses that look like dwarf aircraft hangars with chimneys, to where the trees grow sparse, then we give up. Around here windscreens smash and chip with monotonous regularity thanks to logging trucks coming south, prompting a new game that involves marking the cracks every night and seeing where they migrate to the next morning. Nights are spent with random drunks in places invaria-bly called 'Cocktail Lounge' whose only 'cocktail' is made with a rag in the neck and is prefixed with 'Molotov'. I'm not saying it's rough, but you'd have to be really, really into snowmo-biling not to get murderously bored.

Finally, after an indeterminate time in some almost lethally pretty country-side, we arrive in Inuvik and are met by our Inuvaluit guide who's going to take us to Tuk. He's called, oddly, Dennis.

Mooch out of town, down a small track, and you emerge onto one of the most breathtaking pieces of highway anywhere in the world. It's a 150ft-wide horizontal piste of ice and snow carved into the frozen river. Six-foot-high riverbanks flank a gently curving arc of white three or four hundred feet away, the occasional tree or island lumping up through the ice. There isn't really any need for a speed limit out here, the only advice being to keep to the greyish, bare ice in the middle of the 'road'.

Apparently, running on ice actually warms up tyres for more grip; roll through the powder on the edges of the main roadway and tyres cool so much that you slide around more, though that's a relative amount when you realise that 'slide' becomes a steady state option rather than something you visit from time to time. You learn to handle a bit looser in these conditions and not react to every small movement as you might on tarmac. You literally learn a whole new way of driving in about 20 minutes.

Initially, the Commander flickers all sorts of small traction-control lights until you get to a decent cruising speed, only tickling the ABS around corners taken at a scarcely credible 80mph. On ice. Corners are languor-ous and long, but switch off the electronic fairies and you soon find out that drifting a truck is a strangely graceful experience. The only noise is that of the 5.7-litre Hemi engine grumbling sedately and the faint swoosh of powder snow on tyres.

If you've ever sliced through fresh powder on skis or snowboard, you'll know what I mean. Except in a car it's like meditation: picking out a white road against a background of slightly less white whiteness requires concen-tration, but the lack of background noise and other traffic allows your mind to empty of all unnecessary thought. Soon, idle chat dies in the cabin and you all just end up looking through the battle-scarred windscreen like it's the best movie you've ever seen. In some ways, it is.

The cars kick up rooster tails of snow that fall to the ground in a different way to water, which has a deeper romance with gravity. Snow sparkles

'You just end up looking through the windscreen like it's the best movie you've ever seen'

and floats, making the journey more than a little ethereal. At the halfway point, a small island called Mercy, Dennis tells us that we've crossed onto the Arctic and we are now, technically, an ocean-going Jeep. It doesn't look much different – a few more bumps maybe, a few more pot-holes marked out by little orange cones, but essentially the same. Dennis tells us that he makes the same journey in summer in his boat – except that it takes three or four hours. We've done it in under two on the ice.

Those two hours bring us to the near-mythical Tuktoyaktuk, the most northerly point we can get to. We are introduced to the Inuvaluit way of life by James and Maureen, a mixed-race couple (Maureen is white and from Saskatchewan, James is an Inuvaluit from Tuk) for whom life is a subsistence affair by choice. They hunt for food, rather than buying it. Maureen has cooked us up some whalemeat (fishy black pudding) and I try my hand at blubber (potted ham with jelly), while everyone else tries some dried fish. Fortified by the extra warmth of *mukluk* (cured blubber), Maureen dresses me up in traditional Caribou clothing and polar bear mittens and sends me out to pet the dog team smelling, judging by the reaction, like a really sexy bitch.

Much general amusement (on the part of others) later, we visit the varied sights of this most upwards of places. There's the 1,000 residents (250 of them children; long nights in the Arctic), and lots of outdoorsy activities going on like hunting, fishing and snowmobiling. Plus there's lots of snow and more of the practical-but-nasty-looking shed-houses. Then Maureen takes us to her 'community freezer' – a 30-foot deep warren of tunnels dug straight into the permafrost in which the local families keep food. Behind each and every door is Disney's charnel house: a variety of fish and geese lie flash-frozen with what looks like expressions of gentle panic, but they've got bugger all on the trio of dead seals piled like enormous, flat sausages behind door number two, or the pile of caribou heads and legs in locker four, like a parts bin for big deer. Better warn Bambi that if he ever comes here without an armoured car and body-guards, he's pretty much screwed. I start to look at Maureen in a different light.

On the hill just outside of town there's a pair of those golf-ball satellite protection housings and a load of very military-looking bunkers. I'd like to say they loom, but they don't do anything as impressive – they just sort of squat like geometric fungus. These, James explains, are what's left of the

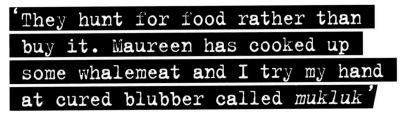

'They hunt for food rather than buy it. Maureen has cooked up some whalemeat and I try my hand at cured blubber called *mukluk*'

American DEWS (Defence Early Warning System) set-up that was supposed to warn of incoming missiles from Russia, in case they decided to chuck a couple over the top. It doesn't seem weird to James. They're just here. This is a man who hunts for his food and makes his own clothes, and he doesn't find the situation odd at all. These electronic eyes don't ever blink; all automated, unmanned, ready to start screaming electronic blue-bloody-murder if anything with a rocket engine so much as farts its way over the tundra. And here we are in a few modern Jeeps thinking we're going to be all cutting edge cyborg to the natives. At least James thinks they look nice in black. I thought I was gadget-heavy, but I haven't got Skunkworks stealth listening equipment in my back garden. Or at least I don't think I do.

After a bit we go and park the Commander on a little jetty that points out into the frozen ocean proper. It's a sobering thought that this is as far as it gets north-wise. In front is 15 miles of frozen ice, a bit of very nearly frozen water and then, the polar ice cap. For a while I just stand and stare out at the grey and white horizon, marvelling at the honking great expanse of nothing stretched arms-wide in front of me. We've driven here without pause for serious thought, up a road made out of frozen mist to find the people here in a very strange situation, with a very strange outlook. Nobody seems to mind that the American military has an installa-tion slap bang next to a family that still dries Caribou skins on their washing line. Where people get the right hump is with Greenpeace who are telling them what they can and cannot eat. Those whales that you subsist on? Not fair game any more. Here, eat this canned junk.

It's all driving home the point that this is a neverwhere place, only accessible if you really want to find it, where normal service is suspended for the time being. Where straight '06 rules don't really apply. You might be able to get here in a relatively normal vehicle, but this is a seriously magical place. Which is why it's fitting that I'm driving home on a road that, come summer, will disappear.

10 9 8 7 6 5 4 3 2 1

Published in 2008 by BBC Books, an imprint of Ebury Publishing.
A Random House Group Company

Anthology copyright © Woodlands Books Ltd 2008
Text copyright © Top Gear magazine 2008
Foreword © copyright Jeremy Clarkson 2008

Photographers: Alex P, Anton Watts, Barry Hayden, James Bareham, Lee Brimble, Mark
Bramley, Stephen Perry, Tom Salt

Writers: Alistair Weaver, Bill Thomas, Emma Parker Bowles, James May, Matt Master
Michael Harvey, Pat Devereux

All rights reserved. No part of this publication may be reproduced, stored in a retrieval system,
or transmitted in any form or by any means, electronic, mechanical, photocopying, recording
or otherwise, without the prior permission of the copyright owner.

The Random House Group Limited Reg. No. 954009

Addresses for companies within the Random House Group can be found at
www.randomhouse.co.uk

A CIP catalogue record for this book is available from the British Library.

ISBN 9781846074646

The Random House Group Limited makes every effort to ensure that the papers used in our
books are made from trees that have been legally sourced from well-managed and credibly
certified forests. Our paper procurement policy can be found on www.randomhouse.co.uk

Commissioning editor: Lorna Russell
Design and Art Direction by: Charlie Turner
Production controller: Antony Heller

Colour origination by Christopher Rowles
Printed and bound in Germany by Firmengruppe APPL, aprinta druck, Wemding